Adult Children, Adult Choices

Outgrowing Codependency

Mary Ramey

Sheed & Ward

Sheed & Ward™ is a service of The National Catholic Reporter
Publishing Company.

Library of Congress Cataloguing-in-Publication Data

Ramey, Mary, 1951-
     Adult children, adult choices : outgrowing codependency /
 Mary Ramey.
         p.   cm.
     Includes bibliographical references.
     ISBN 1-55612-406-6 (acid-free)
         1. Codependency. 2. Codependents—Rehabilitation.
 3. Emotional maturity.   I. Title.
 RC569.5.C63R35   1992
 616.86—dc20   92-12728
                                                             CIP

Published by: Sheed & Ward
                115 E. Armour Blvd.
                P.O. Box 419492
                Kansas City, MO 64141-6492
To order, call: (800) 333-7373

Contents

For my father,

a talented man who taught me

more than he realized

Acknowledgments

Truth is universal by nature, but only sometimes do we get to glimpse a part of it. One glimpse we have is in the statement by authors that there are many, many people to thank as a result of preparing a manuscript for publication, and that they can never all be named, nor thanked enough. Let me take a stab at it anyway.

My family has been very supportive throughout the work of writing, ranging from my husband's agreement for me to cut back my hours of employment as a therapist so that I could write, to the kids not bothering me while I was at the computer unless it constituted a dire emergency. My husband David and my children Matthew, Paul, Andrew, and Elizabeth are the most important people in my life, and I thank them for not only what they do but who they are.

My clients from community mental health settings and from workshops over the years have honored me by sharing the stories of their lives with me, as we worked at identifying what was going wrong and making it as right as possible. We have laughed and cried together, and exchanged the gift of deep personal presence. This book is for them, and I hope it is helpful.

The many authors and teachers I have learned from over my lifetime have shaped the way I think about my experiences and those that others have shared with me. I can never list them all, nor their exact contributions. I hold them in highest regard and deep appreciation.

Others have played a more direct role in preparing this book for publication. Richard Koerner, Psy.D. and Stephen W. Emerick, Ph.D., read versions of the manuscript and made many helpful suggestions. Any errors which remain are my responsibility and not theirs. David Ramey and Virginia Hollenkamp gave me feedback on readability and usefulness.

My colleagues at Eastway Corporation were not only highly supportive, but helped me clarify my thinking through our discussions of cases and theories. The Yellow Springs Women's Research Group provided much-needed enthusiasm and support, and some delicious lunches. Paul Ramey helped me master the computer so that I could get it to print out what I had entered, and so the publishers could access it too.

I am very grateful for all their help, as well as to my friends who were foolhardy enough to ask, "So what's your book about, anyway?" and got an earful. Their interest and encouragement helped me get past the times when I was overwhelmed by the presumption of this project. Thank you all.

Introduction

Codependency is not forever.

There you have, in a nutshell, the major idea of this book. I believe that codependent behaviors can be outgrown and eventually discarded, like other items which serve a practical purpose at one time but at some point lose their effectiveness and are no longer useful. Codependent actions are normal and appropriate human behaviors in certain circumstances and at certain ages, but present a big problem under other conditions. If we understand the whole picture, find out what we could be doing as adults which is more helpful than the codependent stuff, and work at gaining those skills, we don't have to remain codependent. It's that simple.

I became interested in the subject of codependency through my work as a therapist, first working with children in foster care and their families, and later seeing clients at a community mental health center. Most of my clients fit the classical definition of adult children: adults who had grown up in alcoholic homes. I also worked with their children, their siblings, their parents, their spouses. Many had suffered severe additional trauma besides their status as codependents: sexual abuse, physical abuse, poverty, injury or poor health, disrupted schooling. When a colleague introduced me to the concept of codependency, I immediately wanted to learn more about it so that I could understand my clients better and be of greater service to them.

As I read just about every source I came across, I became more and more dissatisfied with what I was reading. The literature did a good job of describing the behaviors of an adult child and what it feels like to be codependent, but there didn't seem to be any way to make sense of what was happening or of how my clients had gotten locked into these patterns in the first place. The behaviors were commonplace, but they seemed to be random; the books would assert that not every adult child displayed every behavior, but that they probably would have at least a majority of the listed characteristics. I wanted to know the bigger picture, and whether it would be possible to predict who would develop what behavior patterns. Also, according to the literature, there was no way to account for the few clients I was seeing who had had horrendous childhoods but were doing a terrific job of making the best of tremendous disadvantages in their adult lives, despite their early experiences.

As I read and discussed the literature with my colleagues who were working with clients with similar backgrounds, I began to notice myself consistently reacting to the various items in the lists of codependent characteristics in the same way: "Well, gee, any kid does that—sounds like a typical adolescent to me—that's normal behavior for a nine-year-old." Things began to make sense when I stopped trying to invent a disease for what I was seeing and began comparing my clients' behaviors with normal human behavior, usually behaviors that were appropriate for someone much younger than my clients' actual ages. My clients responded enthusiastically to the information I began to share with them about how people grow and develop, and how to identify and learn the skills they needed in order to catch up with themselves.

Another concern my clients would bring to the therapy process which really struck me was their feeling of being helpless to make any lasting changes in their lives, and their assumption that they were at the mercy of their early (or current) circumstances. They didn't believe that they had the right to make choices for themselves; or, if they did choose, that the thing they chose would really happen. Over and over, I would assure them, "You're a grown-up; you get to pick." Over and over again they were amazed and delighted when they did choose a course of action and worked to put it into practice, and their lives and relationships got better. It was scary for them not to accept the safety of apparent helplessness, but intensely rewarding when they chose and acted responsibly.

What really upset me, however, was watching intelligent, courageous, highly effective people catch themselves in a less-than-perfectly-mature action, or admit that they were related to a chemically dependent person, and then publicly condemn themselves as hopelessly sick and dysfunctional. The literature insisted that "something happened" to children of alcoholics or of other dysfunctional families, and I would see my clients and my friends practically turn themselves inside out looking for that tragic circumstance or fatal flaw. If they couldn't find one, they would assume that they were in denial and therefore even sicker than they had thought. It got so that they would almost feel guilty for loving someone despite his or her imperfections, or for having happy memories. I was convinced that there had to be a better way of understanding codependency than the disease model; one that would fit the facts more accurately and offer more hope to adult children.

I went back to the models of normal childhood development in various areas of personality: thinking, feeling, making choices. I wanted to see whether the behaviors we label as codependent fit into that framework somehow. When I lined up the lists of codependent characteristics with the stages of development, it was almost a perfect match. Instead of random sick behavior, these actions were the results of trying to cope with the complexity of adult problems while being limited to only child-sized awareness and skills. Getting "stuck" at one level of development in thinking or relating resulted in predictable kinds of unhelpful behaviors; being stuck at a different level resulted in different behaviors that caused other problems but were no less predictable. Now I had a blueprint for where my clients were coming from and I would be able to tell what each individual had to focus on learning in order to catch up with himself or herself as an adult.

The proof of the pudding was that it worked. Clients got past their codependent actions and found better ways of coping with uncomfortable situations. Their lives did not suddenly become serene or problem-free, but now they had more understanding of where they and their feelings were coming from, and so had a better basis for making conscious choices instead of getting pushed around by events. They felt more in charge of their lives and their decisions, and less at the mercy of circumstances. They were more effective in their relationships and in their jobs, and felt much happier as a result. And, as they understood the big picture of development, they could find out for themselves where they were bogged down and what to do about it, instead of waiting for me as the outside authority to tell them what to do.

One thing about working in community mental health— you never have a shortage of clients. I was happy working with my caseload of about 40 clients at any given time, but there were always many more clients than could be seen immediately. Then too, I don't believe that everybody needs to work directly with a therapist in order to solve problems; there are many other kinds of resources to turn to for help. If 90+% of us are codependent, I know that there are many people who are suffering and yet have no idea where to turn to make things better. I wanted to write about what I had learned with my clients about codependency, where it really comes from and how to get out of it. I wanted to be able to share with other adult children who may not have found an effective answer for their concerns as yet.

The result was this book. I hope it is helpful for anyone who recognizes himself or herself as codependent, and would like to get off that merry-go-round. I hope it is useful for counselors and therapists who would like to be of lasting help to their clients who are adult children. I hope it provides a bridge between those in the chemical dependency field and those who study psychology, since sometimes they seem to be talking past each other when really both fields have much to offer those who struggle with compulsive behavior and impaired relationships. I hope it points the way to other sources for unraveling codependency.

I firmly believe that we can outgrow codependency and be done with it. I have seen it happen. When it comes to shaping our lives, we've got a choice—and don't let anybody tell you differently.

Mary Ramey
December 1991

— 1 —

What's the Matter, You Sick?

Codependency. Like the weather, everybody knows what it is, but nobody knows where it comes from or what to do about it. Most writers in the field of substance abuse, where the term was first used, call it an "addiction" or dependence on a harmful circumstance (usually a relationship) which gets in the way of a person's ability to have a healthy, productive life. That is, a codependent person is using a relationship—most likely with someone who is chemically dependent—in order to define himself or herself and to structure the way he or she relates to the rest of the world.

Melody Beattie itemizes nearly 100 characteristics to describe a codependent person in her bestseller on the topic. Janet Woititz lists 13 and Claudia Black lists 15 primary features to help define the codependent behavior of those who grew up in alcoholic homes, although their lists are not exactly the same. Among the commonly accepted features of codependency are telling lies without cause, denying your feelings, trying to control others, having trouble seeing the boundaries between yourself and others, walking away from problem situations instead of trying to solve them, and taking action without thinking about the consequences. There is no one set pattern of characteristics, however, that defines codependency for everyone or that every codependent adult displays, which can be pretty frustrating when we're trying to understand the term. The experts say that their lists show representative behaviors, but that almost nobody will be doing all of them; and there doesn't seem to be any way to predict which person will be acting in which way at what time or in what situation. We're left with the standard that if you show half or more of the behaviors in any given list, you're probably codependent. Some authors

1

seem to imply that you're codependent if you think you are, no matter how many characteristics you think apply to you.

The Disease Model

Since the concept of codependency started within treatment programs for alcoholism and other kinds of chemical dependency, it often uses the same basic set of ideas. The key to this model is that codependency, like dependence on chemicals, is a disease—in this case, a disease of the person who is involved with someone who abuses chemicals. Through their dependence on the addicted person, they become co-dependent on the chemical abuse, or at least on the sickness of the chemically addicted person. This happens no matter what the nature of their relationship is, whether the chemically addicted person is the codependent's parent, spouse, friend, employer, or whatever. The relationship does not even have to be still going on. Adults who grew up in families that included one or more chemically dependent members often continue to display codependent behaviors even after their relationship with the addicted person has been cut off, by choice or by circumstance such as the death of the addict.

Since family members of a chemically addicted person are the ones who have the most close contact with him or her, and therefore are the ones most likely to have a codependent relationship with him or her, some researchers and therapists have taken a look at the families of addicts. They found that often these families already had poor patterns of relating to each other, long before any family member had developed an addiction, and then kept these same poor patterns even if the chemically dependent person stopped using chemicals. In fact, experience shows that in many families when one person stops abusing their chosen drug—alcohol, marijuana, crack, speed, whatever—someone else in the family will start another addiction of some kind, to the same substance or to a different one. Meanwhile, the codependent, "unhealthy" patterns in the family continue.

Further, the fact that some addictions like alcoholism seem to run in families may have a lot to do with these codependent attitudes. People who have grown up in homes where members have abused chemicals often seek partners who already have or will later develop an addiction too. Or, in another common pattern, they find codependent partners who will cover for the addictive behavior that they themselves may develop. This happens even if there have been no signs of addictive behavior in either partner at the time of the marriage, or when the new partner doesn't know about the family's troubled history.

Other families which do not contain any member who uses chemicals in excessive amounts nevertheless have been found to show some of the same kinds of problems that families of chemically dependent persons do. This pattern came to light as therapists and other professionals began identifying and working with adults who had grown up in homes with alcoholic parent figures, and who were finding themselves having problems with relationships and with decisionmaking in their adult lives. The researchers found the problem behaviors and patterns described as codependency among these adults, as one might expect. But then, other clients who had grown up in homes with no history of substance abuse (but with family patterns involving other kinds of compulsive or destructive behaviors such as compulsive gambling, workaholism, or overemphasis on food and eating) seemed to show the same kinds of codependency problems in their lives. The same relationship and self-esteem issues were present; the substance abuse wasn't, at least not in the family history, although sometimes the clients themselves might have begun using some type of drug for a short time before coming into psychotherapy.

This codependent pattern shows up so often in troubled families even when there is no chemical dependency present that many therapists now speak of working with "adult children of dysfunctional families" rather than "adult children of alcoholics," which was the original, more narrow term. This shift of language enlarges the focus beyond just the role of chemical abuse within a person's life experiences to that person's overall family behavior patterns instead.

Yet this shift from thinking about codependency as based on chemical dependency to considering it as a problem within persons or families has been incomplete. Underneath the new person-oriented words, therapists are stuck with using disease as the main model for their work with codependent individuals and families. The fact that disease and chemical addiction (which is a physical condition at least in part) are still the basic mindsets which are used to think about codependency, regardless of whether chemical dependency is present in the family or not, becomes clear from the way these therapists speak about dysfunctional families.

Dysfunctional means something that doesn't work well or perform properly. Yet when the experts contrast the ways these families function with a better way to operate, they don't use words which describe efficiency or harmony. They use the term "healthy," a word which makes us think of the physical state of wellness. Just like those who work directly with drug-dependent people, therapists working with adult children freely use words like "sick," "addicted," "recovery," and "disease," all of which call up images of medicine or hospitals or some physical problem.

Now, it's clear that chemical dependency does have a physical factor to consider. Recent studies have suggested that some people inherit a particular sensitivity to alcohol or cocaine that increases the chances that their bodies will have even more difficulty dealing with these substances than the rest of us might. This seems to be true for about one-quarter to one-third of those persons, especially males, who can be called chemically dependent. (Interestingly, these percentages just about match the percentage of people who find Alcoholics Anonymous ineffective in helping them stay away from using alcohol.) And of course since chemicals themselves are physical substances, they always have physical effects on our bodies. Each chemical has its own set of effects, and if two or more chemicals are present at the same time (alcohol and nicotine, for example, or amphetamines and barbiturates) a variety of things can happen:

— They can work together to make each one stronger than it would have been alone.

— Each can work in opposite ways so that normal body processes are thrown dangerously out of balance.

— They can even cause some entirely new reaction that neither chemical could have caused by itself.

But we're talking about codependent people, not chemically dependent people, and codependency does not necessarily mean that the codependent person is using a chemical. What's the problem with using a physical or medical image like disease or addiction to describe codependency, if it helps make clear what is going on? The problem is that it really doesn't make things clear if it doesn't fit the facts. Many experts on codependency accept John and Linda Friel's estimate that as many as 90% or more of us are codependent, as we described the behaviors and circumstances earlier. If they are correct, and they well may be, then does using a disease model really fit anymore? You might as well call changing your mind a disease, or having gray hair or wrinkles—they might not be pleasant experiences, but they aren't unusual or even necessarily a warning that anything is wrong. And if practically all of us are sick, then where are all these "healthy" people and families that are offered as the ideal model by those who work in the fields of substance abuse and codependency? Do these charmed healthy 10% of us ever act dependent or destructive? How did they manage to escape or become immune to infection? How can any of the rest of us ever get well if we're always going to be surrounded by others who are sick too? These questions are difficult to deal with if we insist on using the disease model for understanding codependency.

The disease model of alcoholism and chemical dependency came about as a reaction to earlier kinds of thinking about people who abused drugs. Before this current school of thought was commonly accepted, which has happened in the past thirty years or so, a lot of shame and contempt and blame was heaped on drinkers (as well as on users of other drugs). They were seen as weak-willed, lily-livered lightweights or stubborn, self-seeking sinners or crazy or possessed by demons or just plain wrong. None of this blaming helped anybody stop drinking or using other chemicals, and in fact probably made things worse.

Using disease as a way to think about substance abuse cut through this blaming and shame, and helped people focus on drinking as the problem, not the drinker himself. Just as society wouldn't condemn someone for having measles but would offer them help instead, so alcoholics and nonalcoholics alike were able to focus on getting help instead of getting blamed. It also helped us to get used to thinking about using or not using chemicals as a process over time, not as a once-and-for-all absolute. These have been valuable gains in making successful treatment possible for chemically-abusing people. For these people, who are in fact altering their physical condition when they use chemicals, the disease model can be a useful one. It's still only a model, however: a mock-up, a way of thinking about facts to help us put them together in a way that makes sense. A model is not a fact itself, but a way of arranging ideas about facts so that we can possibly find some useful way to deal with them.

Trying to make a model based on a physical problem fit a nonphysical problem like codependency is less helpful. One of the basic assumptions built into a disease framework is that a primary task for dealing with the disease will be to remove the source of the infection or contamination. This is obviously going to be pretty hard to do if 9 out of 10 people we come into contact with are carriers of the illness. Or maybe even a higher percentage will be diseased, since it is reasonable to suppose that "healthy" families would look to each other for support and try to avoid the rest of us as sources of infection.

Another difficulty with using the disease model as the way to think about codependency is the problem of staying motivated to make changes when you see yourself as chronically ill, or at least in an unending recovery with no real possibility of cure. We are accustomed to thinking of diseases as being curable, especially with the aid of science and technology. Labeling ourselves (and most everyone we know) as sick can lead to a "what's the use" attitude which can actually work against recovery. Patients with chronic physical illnesses often have to fight long and hard against this threat of hopelessness as their illness lingers on and on; a less specific chronic "illness" like codependency is perhaps even more likely to cause discouragement and despair, especially when there's nothing physical to fight or to use as a weapon.

So if using the disease model for thinking about codependency doesn't work, is our only alternative a return to the bad old days of blame and condemnation? Or perhaps we should just give up altogether: "I'm codependent; so what?" Not necessarily, but we need a more useful way of thinking about codependency, a way which preserves the gains of the disease model but avoids its problems. Perhaps things would be clearer if we think of codependency not as a process of disease but as one of development.

Another Look at Codependency

Many of the behavior patterns of codependency can be looked at as distortions or short-circuits of processes which are a normal part of ordinary human development. For example, everyone is familiar with the constant "no!"—even when she means "yes"—of the toddler as she struggles to get her way, and we've all seen the way teenagers tie themselves into knots worrying about the opinions of other kids, doing foolish or even dangerous things to try to gain acceptance. All of us display these and other less-than-ideal behaviors at certain times of our lives, as a normal part of growing up.

Sometimes, however, we can get stuck in certain behaviors and we may not develop the next set of skills, or the next higher understanding of how something works, or the next level of awareness of ourselves and others. This can happen to anybody, but it may be a particular problem for children of dysfunctional families, who don't have strong role models to show them the behaviors, attitudes and skills available at later levels of emotional or social development. When we don't move ahead in our development—and this can happen for a number of reasons—we try to use lower-level solutions for problems which are really too complex for them to be able to work well. It's kind of like trying to use a toy piano to compose a symphony—it certainly has something to do with the task, but we're not going to get very far if that's all we have to work with. Using inadequate skills or solutions for adult problems can complicate these problems even further, contributing to the bigger, more complex, problem-causing patterns of behavior which we group together under the label of codependency.

If we look at codependency from this perspective it takes on a whole different significance. Instead of being the result of a physical addiction, whether it's my own addiction or someone else's, what we call codependent behavior may in fact be what contributes to the development of an addiction in the first place. Codependent—that is, lower-level or underdeveloped—attitudes and actions lead to inadequate responses to problem situations, and may even set the stage for eventually using a drug as an attempt to cope with the panic or the frustration. Or sometimes we may keep trying over and over to apply a simple solution to a complex problem, even when it's not working or is actually making things worse, because it seemed to help in the beginning. The less it helps, the more we stick with it because we don't know what else to do, and we're scared to quit trying to use it because that might be even worse.

Looking at codependency from a developmental standpoint, and as a possible cause of addiction rather than a result of it, also may help shed some light on the reason that not all substance abusers become truly addicted. There are thousands of people who abuse drugs or alcohol for a certain limited period of time, then never overuse them again and go on to lead highly productive lives. Perhaps their "disease" went into remission; if so, why? And how? And why doesn't everyone else's? The questions come thick and fast, and are difficult to answer with the disease model. It seems far simpler to suggest that these people were able to develop the skills to address the problems they were having in more creative, constructive ways and so leave behind their less mature attempts at solutions. They may learn about better choices and how to make them (such as in a 12-step program), or perhaps they remember skills they once had but have not been using. Quite simply, maybe they've grown beyond the place where they've been stuck—and if they can manage to do this, perhaps the rest of us could too.

This concept for codependency also fits the millions of us who grew up in dysfunctional families but never develop a dependency on drugs or alcohol. Do we become "addicted" to shopping or food or sex in the same way that we become physically dependent on chemicals? If so, how are we able to change the pattern or content of our addictions from one kind of problem to another so easily? Do we "catch" the new addiction from companions? What keeps us from becoming addicted to almost everything, the way a chronically ill person becomes more susceptible to other diseases as his immune system gradually breaks down? Why aren't all of us eventually drug-dependent?

A mindset that focuses on developmental issues makes sense of this more easily. Normal human development is not always smooth. Growth spurts explode in infancy, then slow down during the rest of childhood until they speed up again during adolescence. Physical growth may slack off a bit for a short time while mental skills rapidly expand. We develop different skills at different times in our lives, depending on factors like heredity, readiness, and circumstances in our environment. We also differ in the levels of our abilities in various areas of our lives: we might be great at math but barely adequate in spelling. An individual might be able to communicate beautifully onstage or in a professional setting, but fall apart when trying to make casual conversation one-to-one at a party. Furthermore, not everybody develops all of the same capabilities in the same way even under what look like the same circumstances. One person in a family may be physically gifted while another is talented artistically and a third is an organizational genius. Just because we're members of one family doesn't mean we're cookie-cutter duplicates. Our development is the result of a mixture of our inner individual resources and our outer environment, so everyone comes out just a little bit different.

A careful look at some of the major issues in ordinary human development may help us understand where and how codependent people may have gotten stuck or sidetracked along the way. That is the focus of this book: to outline several issues in turn and examine both the normal expected path of development as well as how to "catch up," if for some reason a person's social or emotional development has been slowed or stopped in one or more areas—such as may happen in a dysfunctional family. It helps us put codependent behaviors into the context of normal human behavior and development. If the vast majority of us are codependent for some reason, as the experts suggest, then surely codependency must have something to do with normal development, or else development isn't really "normal"—that is, the thing which happens most often to the most people in whatever group one is talking about (the more technical definition of *normal*)—after all.

Developmental psychology looks at human growth from the point of view that each of us is trying to strike a balance between ourselves and our surroundings in order to function at our best. Sometimes we're successful at setting and keeping this balance, and our lives run pretty smoothly for a while. At other times, something within ourselves changes—we get older, or bigger, or stronger, or smarter—and we begin to change how we react to our environment because of this. Or something in the environment changes—a new baby in the family, a serious illness, a new job or home—and we have to change in order to deal with the new circumstances. The changes that occur come from our attempts to get back into balance with our surroundings again.

The research that has been done on human development has shown that certain patterns seem to hold true for how we grow and change. It indicates that growth and maturation take place in stages, whether we're talking about physical, mental, emotional, or social growth. We don't just suddenly leap ahead willy-nilly in some area; the changes proceed in an orderly fashion, and we can predict what they will be to a reasonable degree of accuracy.

There are four assumptions about stages of human development that seem to be true so far as we have been able to test them. First, stages of development are *hierarchical*: each new stage builds on the one which came before it. Second, stages are *sequential*: they come in a logical order, not in a random, unpredictable way. Third, stages are *invariant*: we can't skip any of them, they have to be worked through in order. Fourth, stages of development seem to be *universal*: they seem to hold true for people despite differences in gender, culture, religion, nationality, and so forth, as far as we can tell from studies which have tried to take these things into account.

One other characteristic of the stage theory of human development is important to remember. Completing the work of one stage is necessary in order to go to the next one, but it is not the whole story. In other words, if I have learned all the skills and completed all the growth of whatever stage I am currently in, I am then ready to move on. This is no guarantee that I will automatically go on ahead with my growth, however. I may just stay where I am, and use the skills I have already learned to try to maintain that balance between myself and my environment. I could continue to grow, but I might choose not to, for any number of reasons. It's not an automatic process, especially at the higher levels of development. We have to choose to work at it.

This may be what happens to those of us who consider ourselves codependent. We seem to have gotten stuck in our progress through the stages of development, in one or more areas of our lives. Something is holding us back from moving on to the next level of ability in relationships or feelings or work or self-esteem or whatever. We need to find out where we're stuck, what the next stage is, and how to get there. Fortunately, road maps are available, if we just know where to look. Unlike the disease model, which says "not every codependent person will have all 13 (or 15 or 96) of these characteristic problems, but they will definitely have most of them, only we can't tell which ones you will have for sure ahead of time," the developmental model can give us a fairly definite idea of what kinds of issues or behaviors will be a problem at each particular stage, how to get out of being stuck there, and what to expect next as we move on.

There's another piece of good news built into the developmental model for adult children of dysfunctional families and other codependent adults who want to work at catching up with themselves. During childhood and adolescence, when we first get the opportunity to move from stage to stage in the various areas of human development, sometimes our growth has to wait for our physical maturity to take place. For example, nobody, no matter how creative or intelligent they might be, seems to be capable of what we call formal logical thought ("If *a* is true and *b* is true, then *c* must be false") until about the age of 12 or so. Our brains seem to need that much time to develop all the necessary neurological connections in order for this kind of thinking to be possible. Once we have reached our full physical maturation, however—that is, once we have grown to physical adulthood—we don't have to wait for our bodies to catch up with us anymore in order to grow and improve our skills. We may be able to make much more rapid progress through the stages of development than we might have as kids because of already being physically grown up. We still will need to go through the stages of human development in their regular order, but it won't have to take us another 18 years to do it if we're actively working at it as adults.

All of us clearly have had at least some success in growth and development, or else we never would have learned so much as how to roll over. Surely we have the potential to work toward continuing our development, at least to whatever limits we may have physically or genetically. Overcoming codependency then becomes not a matter of recovery from an illness, but a matter of learning, something which is certainly possible and open to everyone to at least some degree—or so we've always assumed, since we used that as the basis for setting up our national system of public education.

Of course, learning and education are never perfect or complete; who can know everything there is to know? However, it's not necessary to know everything in order to be able to see progress or improvement in one's situation. Learning even one skill you didn't have before can have an immediate impact on your life—just ask the kid who recently learned how to turn the knob and open the door! The more you practice a skill, the more a part of you it becomes and the easier it is to call it up and use it when needed. And the more skills we possess, the more freedom we have in choosing how and when to act.

Looking at codependency in this developmental learning context gives a far more hopeful picture than the disease model presents. We are not diseased, but unfinished. We are not defective, just in need of a better idea than the low-level skill we're trying to apply at the moment. We are not chronically ill or stuck in everlasting recovery; we have loads of possibilities and choices that we haven't yet explored, much less made use of.

It is the issue of choices that becomes central when thinking about codependency from this perspective. Much of the current information on codependency-as-a-disease, as it considers the various aspects of recovery, mentions almost in passing that as dependent people get better they "recover their choices." It may be more to the point to focus on choices and decision-making as the heart of the matter. People who are addicted don't see themselves as having any choice about it. Compulsive behavior is activity that someone does even when he or she doesn't want to. Many times people honestly don't know any other way to respond to a problem except to drink (smoke, take pills, shop; fill in the blank with any "addiction"). Or, if they do hear about another way to respond, they don't know how to go about doing it because they never learned or have forgotten how.

If we can become aware of our options, we don't have to be locked into just one answer for a problem anymore. If we can learn several ways to deal with a situation—ways that don't cause harm to ourselves or to others—then the power of the old unhelpful solutions is weakened. If we can educate ourselves and each other, we don't have to remain codependent. Or we can take a look at the amount of effort and energy involved in continuing to grow past the place we got stopped in our development and say, "No thanks, I'll stay where I am. It stinks, but at least it's familiar." It's up to us—we've got a choice.

"I Won't Grow Up"

I won't grow up
I don't want to go to school
Just to learn to be a parrot
And recite some silly rule.
If growing up means it would be
Beneath my dignity to climb a tree
I'll never grow up
Never grow up
Never grow up
Not me.

I won't grow up
I don't want to wear a tie
And a serious expression
In the middle of July.
And if it means I must prepare
To shoulder burdens with a worried air
I'll never grow up
Never grow up
Never grow up
Not me.
(Not I.)
Not me—so there.

Never gonna be a man—I won't!
Like to see somebody try and make me.
Anyone who wants to try and make me
Learn to be a man—
Catch me if you can!

I won't grow up
Not a penny will I pinch.
I will never grow a moustache
Or a fraction of an inch.
'Cause growing up is awfuller
Than all the awful things that ever were.
I'll never grow up
Never grow up
Never grow up
No sir.

Related Readings

Beattie, Melody, *Codependent No More*, New York: Harper/ Hazelden, 1987.

Black, Claudia, *Double Duty*, New York: Ballantine Books, 1990.

Friel, John and Friel, Linda, *Adult Children: The Secrets of Dysfunctional Families*, Pompano Beach, FL: Health Communications Inc., 1988.

Woititz, Janet G., *Adult Children of Alcoholics*, Pompano Beach, FL: Health Communications, Inc., 1983.

— 2 —

I (Don't) Want To Be Alone

It's interesting that we rarely speak of children as being codependent. True, Alcoholics Anonymous for many years has offered Alateen groups for teenaged children who are affected by a relative or friend's drinking, but there are few other kinds of interventions aimed specifically at kids. Many families seek treatment together for chemical dependency or codependency, so that the children get some attention or instruction on the issues of dependency in that way; but the focus even in family therapy is first and foremost on the adults, since they're the ones who set the guidelines and enforce the standards for behavior in the family. The children, even the ones who are causing problems and behaving dangerously, are usually seen as primarily reacting to the messed-up patterns in the family which have been created (or at least permitted) by the adults.

The adults have gotten themselves and their families into this situation because they don't feel able to do what adults do—namely, set the guidelines and enforce the standards of acceptable behavior for family members, including themselves. They still feel like kids inside, wanting direction from somebody else because they don't feel sure of themselves or confident of the answers to the countless questions of daily life. (This very unsureness may be one of the processes which has contributed to chemical abuse or dependence by one or more family members, as they try to deal with the atmosphere of uncertainty and insecurity within the family.)

The children feel the adults' doubtfulness and react to it with anxiety and insecurity of their own. They are not able to watch the adults for clues as to how a grown-up thinks or behaves because the grown-ups themselves often act like kids. So the real kids stay locked into being kids instead of moving forward to develop more adult attitudes and skills for dealing with relationships, work situations, project planning, and other problems of daily life. It's because of this process that the term "adult children" (of dysfunctional families) is so appropriate. It captures not only the literal meaning, people who grew up in a family with specific problems in handling life situations. It also is a good description of how these people feel and sometimes act: like scared kids.

Many of the therapy and support programs as well as the literature for drug-dependent persons and their families encourage getting in touch with or setting free this child within themselves. Perhaps a forgotten piece of recovery is also to educate that child within us, to help the kid in us grow and learn and become more able to care for ourselves and others in helpful ways.

Thinking of ourselves as having a child still inside us even though we are now adults may shed some light on what it means to be codependent. Kids are *childlike*: that is, they are curious, open, energetic, enthusiastic, fun-loving and spontaneous. Kids are also *childish*: impatient, thoughtless, demanding, easily distracted and focused mostly on their own wants and feelings. The task of growing up—that is, of becoming adult— is to keep or expand the childlike qualities within us while learning to lessen or work through the childish ones. Therefore, even a fully adult person still has a lot in common with a child. This has to be true, or else adults and children wouldn't be able to relate to each other long enough and well enough for anybody to grow up and the human race would die out. We try to learn, as we grow, how to keep the helpful skills and attitudes of childhood while we substitute better options for the not-so-helpful ones.

This means that even as adults we can benefit from some awareness of what kids need to learn and to deal with, and how they go about doing this. There are many models of human development that have been suggested by psychologists and psychiatrists and researchers like Freud, Erickson, Miller, Fowler, Levinson, Gilligan, and others. Some of the models describe a particular order in which people deal with various issues as they develop. Others suggest that the timing of developmental issues is strongly influenced by whether someone is male or female; an oldest, youngest or only child; from a particular culture or class; or various other factors.

Some of the models have been so different that you may wonder if the authors are really all trying to describe the same process! No matter how much the specific details of one author's theory may differ from another's, however, there is fairly general agreement on the kinds of questions each of us must face in order to grow up. Perhaps taking a look at these basic human developmental issues—how they crop up in childhood and how we can get stuck in them along the way—can help us understand certain adult problems and behaviors that we've come to call codependent.

One of the most basic and common characteristics of codependency is a fear of being alone or abandoned. This feeling goes far beyond just wanting to have people around. It's a real fear, almost a panic, when the person has to stay by himself or herself for more than a very short time. Or it can show up as a fear of having to make a decision or take some responsibility on one's own without getting someone else involved to share the burden. Codependent people will often go to great lengths to avoid going out on a limb or being left holding the bag—in short, they may avoid any situation that suggests that they are alone.

It's worth noting that the greatest fear reported by children in a recent study of kids under 12 was being left alone (abandoned) by adults. This finding surprised the researchers, who had asked teachers, social workers, school psychologists and other professionals who work with children what they thought the kids would list as their biggest fears. None of the experts had even listed this one, much less put it at the top! When you think about it, though, the findings make a lot of sense. Kids are aware that they don't know everything they need to know, like how to handle an emergency and how to provide what they need. They rely on adults to take care of these things. They don't know how grown-ups know all that stuff (as they mistakenly assume that all adults automatically know how to do all of it), and they're scared that they might have to know it too before they're ready. Kids constantly feel afraid that they won't measure up; and while that's painful but mostly inconvenient on the small scale ("Can I win this game?"), it is intensely scary and intimidating and possibly even dangerous on a large scale ("What if a burglar comes?"). Kids' fears of being abandoned aren't always tied to a specific worry such as fire or being attacked or having enough food. Sometimes it's just a fear of being helpless or forgotten by the ones they depend on, a sort of nightmarish dread that says "Oh no! What if—?" but doesn't dare to finish the question.

Infancy

Fears of being abandoned are easily understandable when we consider how helpless we all start out as infants. Babies are not really all that delicate—the instinct to survive is very strong in a newborn, and babies have managed to live through natural disasters like earthquakes which killed adults around them, for no apparent reason other than the strength of this instinct. But even if they aren't delicate, they still are helpless, and if they can't get food, warmth, shelter and stimulation from someone else, they cannot provide it for themselves. A newborn can barely hold up its head, and just getting its eyes to focus on an object is a major accomplishment. No wonder being abandoned is such a terrible, fearful thing!

Newborns don't realize that they are separate from the world around them and the people in it. They aren't aware of any difference between what they feel inside and what happens outside their bodies, at least as far as we can tell from working with them. (The babies themselves aren't able to tell us directly, of course.) The adults who take care of their needs seem, to babies, to be extensions of themselves, as close and connected to them as a hand or a foot. It takes months for a baby to grow through the process of learning to recognize a particular person (for example, this is Daddy) and then to tell the difference between familiar people and strangers, which babies show by acting shy or scared around people—even relatives—that they don't see often. The process of learning that the people closest to the baby, especially Mommy and Daddy, are not just a part of themselves takes even longer. It lingers over several years and takes place in recognizable stages, including the Terrible Twos and the Ferocious Fours. Certain faint traces of it occur again in later times too, especially during the teenage years.

Physical abandonment poses the greatest risk to a baby, obviously, but emotional absence at this stage in life has serious consequences too. People who don't get enough attention from others during babyhood grow up feeling very scared and dependent and alone. They may cling almost frantically to anyone who will pay attention to them, even as adults, because they are so fearful that the other person is going to disappear without warning the way others seemed to when they were babies. Not having someone around feels as intensely scary now as it did when they really were helpless. And since the original feeling of fear was experienced at a time before the person had grown up enough to have learned how to talk, it may be hard to put this fear into words as an adult so that she or he can deal with it more easily.

The relationships which a person who is still living at this level of fear enters into are as lopsided as a baby's. Just as a baby tries to provoke a response from the people around it by doing whatever it can (smiling, cooing, crying, waving its arms and kicking), so these adults can sometimes seem almost desperate in their efforts to attract attention too. The activities they use are likely to be somewhat different from a baby's, however: telling jokes, showing off their skills or strength, and so on. If others respond to them, they will double and redouble their efforts in order to please their "audience" and get them to stay tuned in, just as a young baby will gurgle at an adult until they get a response. People who are wrestling with a fear this basic feel incomplete in a very real sense unless they have someone they feel they can claim as their own, in a dependence that feels similar in many ways to the natural dependence of babies. They will even put up with abuse from partners just so they do not have to face being alone, because being alone feels like being abandoned, just as it did when they were helpless infants and really were in danger if left unattended for too long.

People who struggle with this fear at this deepest level cling desperately to whatever relationships they have and are very demanding in them. After all, who is more demanding than a baby? They are preoccupied with the need they feel for the other person and can devote almost every waking moment to thinking about him or her as they go through the tasks of their daily life. They may phone several times a day, pop up unexpectedly, send cards or gifts, and find other ways to make their presence felt. They are intensely jealous of anyone or anything which tries to claim the other person's attention even briefly, just as a toddler tries to demand his mother's attention if she starts to become involved in another task or talk to another person (especially, heaven forbid, another baby!). While the friend or lover may appreciate all this attention at first, eventually it becomes as wearing as a baby's constant demands, and troubles start in the relationship as the other person tries to create some space for their own needs and desires.

Issue: abandonment
Level: earliest
Feeling: terror, helplessness
Codependent behaviors: • constant demands for attention • jealous of anything which claims the other's attention

The panic that even this much separation causes in a codependent person who is operating on this very basic level is bad enough, but it intensifies even more when eventually the relationship ends. Ending a relationship, no matter how bad it might have been, feels almost exactly like the original abandonment, and the adult child reacts in almost the same way as an infant: with terror and fury. The feelings seem so overwhelming that the person forgets that he or she has grown up and is no longer helpless. Their desperation at being abandoned by their partner may blind them to the good in other relationships in their lives, as well as to other resources they may already have available for companionship and self-esteem.

Childhood

As babies toddle into childhood and learn to master their muscles, they are no longer as completely helpless as they started. They develop enough skill at controlling their muscles to be able to do a little exploring on their own, although they still need to check in with an adult every little while for reassurance. Being able to do something on your own is a true joy, and toddlers dive into it with eagerness. "I do it!" is not only a good thing in itself, it's a real relief from having to wait for someone else to take care of your needs. The joy of doing for himself or herself, however, sometimes runs ahead of the toddler's ability to actually take care of the task, and parents are forever having to save little ones from hurting themselves as they try to manage an activity that they don't yet have the strength or the skills for.

Parents have a major role in how toddlers work on this issue. Little ones will patiently try over and over to figure out how to do something because it's new to them and therefore interesting to learn. Our brains release pleasure-causing chemicals when we focus our attention to learn something new, which is one of the reasons humans are so naturally curious and eager to learn. An experience of "Aha!" as we figure things out is rewarding not only mentally but physically as well. For the parent, though, the simple tasks with which the toddler is struggling are old news and the adult is usually bored and ready to move on long before the child is.

Dr. Benjamin Spock, world-famous for his interest in children and their development, tells of an episode he had with a baby while he was a young doctor. He wanted to test the baby's attention span, so he gave the baby a key and let her explore it for a few seconds; then he offered her another key. The baby dropped the first key and took the second, and promptly became absorbed in exploring it. After a few seconds, Dr. Spock offered the baby the first key again. The baby promptly dropped the one she had and accepted the "new" key. Dr. Spock kept alternating between the keys, and each time the baby dropped the current one and took the next one offered. After 20 minutes the baby was still happily accepting and exploring keys; Dr. Spock says he was bored silly and wishing he had never started the whole process! It takes people, especially young ones, a long time to master a skill, and the interest which sustains us while we're in the process can drop off dramatically once we're comfortable with our level of accomplishment at it.

Parents may find it hard to be patient while their toddlers practice over and over again on some simple task. The temptation is to jump in and get it done for them so that we can move on to something else. Sometimes this is unavoidable because of the demands of other schedules and tasks. Other times, parents may step in because they fear that the child may get hurt or dirty. But if a parent needlessly prevents the toddler from completing a task and learning that much more about how to use her body or how to care for himself, that old feeling of fear and helplessness lasts longer than it really has to in terms of how human beings grow and develop best.

As children get older, the kinds of tasks they need to learn get more complicated. Kids work at mastering their mental abilities as well as their bodies. They need guidance with these tasks in much the same way that they needed help in learning to roll over or to dress themselves. Even though the tasks are different—or maybe because they are so different—children still feel dependent on adults to teach them, and are afraid of being on their own before they are ready. They look for help, first and foremost, from their parents. If that help isn't available, they may cope in several ways. One, they may seek out another source that seems knowledgeable: another relative, a coach, a teacher, a friend's parent, a neighbor, another kid. Two, they may try to figure it out on their own and/or bluff their way through it. Three, they may throw a tantrum or go back to acting helpless to try to get somebody to do it for them. Four, they may just walk away from the whole uncomfortable situation.

Uncomfortable is a key word in this issue. People who are dealing with abandonment issues are living in fear, which is probably the most uncomfortable emotion to experience. Other emotions such as anger can be unpleasant to experience too, but at least there's a sense of physical power or strength from the rush of adrenaline that anger triggers. Fear feels like the opposite end of the power spectrum: weak, helpless, unprotected, vulnerable, alone. This is highly uncomfortable, and we go to almost any length to avoid it. Figuring that at least there's safety in numbers, we will do nearly anything at times in order to keep from having to be alone.

Consider that the worst punishment we have been able to come up with (short of ending someone's life), the very worst thing that we reserve for convicted felons who break the rules in prison or for prisoners in wartime we are trying to break, is solitary confinement: keeping someone absolutely alone for long periods of time with no human contact. One of the worst things about being held hostage is the fear that those you left behind have forgotten you and are not making efforts to get you back. Abandonment is a very basic human fear, one that strikes at the very foundation of human existence.

So if fear of being alone is so very basic, it follows that we have a pretty strong desire to please others so that they'll be willing to stay with us. Psychologists have long known that the most effective means for changing a child's behavior is withdrawing affection or approval. (In other words, "I won't be your friend anymore.") Even this small degree of "leaving" or withdrawing as the consequence of doing the particular behavior (in this case, whatever it is that the adult doesn't like) is so uncomfortable that the child usually doesn't do it anymore. Kids fear being abandoned more than anything else, so that even a lesser form of abandonment like disapproval is painful enough to cause the child to follow the adult's standards most of the time, especially if the child is still very young.

Children have an especially strong desire and need to please their parents, since parents are so central in a child's life and the child is so dependent on them. Parents use this natural tendency to want to please them within their children as a learning tool, both when they express approval or encouragement for some kinds of behaviors and when they express anger or rejection for other kinds. The more consistent a parent is about which behaviors get which response, the quicker the child learns the rules of acceptable behavior. If the standards aren't clear, or if they aren't enforced pretty much the same way from one time to the next, the child is confused about what pleases the parent and becomes scared to act without a lot of checking and rechecking, since mistakes could cost them the parent's approval or even result in losing the parent's attention or presence. This is particularly frightening for kids because young children find it hard to tell the difference between temporary and permanent abandonment. Since their sense of time is not yet well-developed, any absence of the parent feels permanent until it is over. This pattern of needing constant presence and/or reassurance from others can persist long beyond childhood unless these fears are addressed.

It is in this particular stage of dealing with fears of abandonment that many codependent adults are stuck. Maybe they weren't able to get clear and consistent definitions and enforcement of standards of behavior from adults when they were kids. Maybe they lived through particularly frightening experiences of being helpless: physical or sexual abuse, trying to rouse a drunken unconscious parent, being in accidents or near misses, and so on. Maybe their parents were too preoccupied with other matters—whether legitimate and unavoidable concerns such as a family emergency, or just their own unresolved fears or dependencies—to be present emotionally or physically to their children, and the kids weren't able to find substitute adults to provide nurturing and direction. Whatever the reasons, these codependent adults are now trying to cope with their fears in various life situations by using the same basic tactics a child does, on the same simple level a child does—bluffs, tantrums, anxious rechecking, acting helpless or backing out of the situation. They don't yet have all the information they need about how people operate, or have the problem-solving skills to act like an adult: to set their own guidelines and enforce reasonable standards of behavior. They are acting and feeling like children—adult children.

People who are operating at this level of development tend to worry a great deal about what others think of them and whether they're doing things right. They let others call the shots in a relationship, rather than taking part in setting the limits and standards of behavior for themselves. They ask for lots of reassurance that they are doing okay at meeting others' expectations.

Criticism from anyone else is devastating because it seems like proof that they messed up and have displeased the other person. This of course means that the other person may leave them. Therefore codependents who are stuck at this level judge themselves very harshly to make sure that they catch any mistakes before anybody else has the chance to find them and get mad. They also take responsibility for pleasing the other person so much to heart that they try to anticipate what he or she might want and do it even before they're asked. They are helpful and cheerful to a fault sometimes, and extremely apologetic if the other person finds some reason to get angry anyway.

Sometimes, however, they get tired of being so dependent in a relationship and want to assert some of the skills they have already developed. They may try to get the other person to cater to them for once, to pay back for all the effort they have poured out already on being good. For the most part, though, they shoulder the burden of pleasing everybody whether they want to and whether it's fair (or even possible) or not.

Issue: abandonment
Level: middle
Feelings: • desperate to please • fear of making someone angry
Codependent behaviors: • checking and rechecking standards • constant requests for reassurance • judging self harshly • acting "helpful" before being asked • throwing tantrums

Alternatively, someone at this stage, fearing abandonment, may try to control the other person by means of tantrums or pouting in order to get their attention and ensure that they stay committed to the relationship. Babies are capable of making quite a racket when they are aware of a need which they want met, and we do not necessarily lose this ability as we grow. Adult children may not be convinced of their abilities to meet their own needs, or to find alternate resources for pleasant companionship or intimate relationships, so they grab onto whatever ones they have with an iron fist and use every trick in the book to make sure that the other person knows how central and important they are to daily life. The dominant feeling is "I need you" rather than "I love you" or "I choose you."

Adolescence

As a child grows into adolescence, friends start to replace parents as the ones he or she worries about pleasing. A teenager is not as dependent on adults for care or security as is a younger child, and they're better able to begin to separate mentally as well as physically from being supervised by adults. Fears of being alone, or at least of not being liked or approved of, can still linger nonetheless, although now it's one's friends or gang or clique who set the standards for behavior and enforce them. When you're a teenager, the second worst thing that can happen is that everybody will *look* at you . . . and the worst thing that can happen is that *nobody* will look at you.

So, in a sense, the fear of being alone or abandoned takes another form as we grow. We become a little less worried about being physically alone but more concerned about being disapproved of. One particularly painful experience of this kind of abandonment is being ignored. In fact, being treated as if you weren't even there is so painful that people prefer active disapproval to being passed over. If there's no praise or encouragement available from parents or peers, kids will provoke anger or disapproval, because it's a less scary form of abandonment than being ignored. If we can't get a solid sense of what the rules will permit for acceptable behavior, at least we can find out what isn't allowed. Any response is better than none.

However, our concerns about emotional or social abandonment go beyond mere approval; we want to be liked. We want, in fact, to be special—at least to a particular someone. We begin looking for a person to share our life with, to be closer to than anyone else. We want to have a relationship with someone who will accept our weaknesses as well as our strengths and who we can count on to remain with us. As children, we want this kind of relationship with our family members, especially our parents. As we grow to school age and widen our contacts with people to develop friendships outside our circle of relatives, we try to find one or two "best friends" with whom we feel close and safe emotionally.

In adolescence, sexual feelings begin to surface in these nonfamily relationships. As these feelings combine with our needs for intimacy, our fears of abandonment are experienced and dealt with on a new level. We want a freely chosen love with someone who thinks we're unique and special and important. If we've had the chance to work through the earlier forms of the fear of abandonment, especially the experience of ourselves as totally helpless, we also want to provide this kind of nurturing to that someone, not just receive it from them.

If, on the other hand, we are still struggling with this fear of abandonment on the other levels, it is very difficult to work through it successfully in the area of mutual loving relationships. It's hard to muster the trust we need to let someone close enough to know and love us if we are still very fearful about whether we'll be approved of, helped when we need it but not when we don't, or even abandoned without warning. As we've noted, codependent people have often had poor experiences with the most important people in their childhoods on these issues. They haven't received the consistent, clear messages of love and limits which empower them to quiet the fear and move ahead in their development. So it is that adult relationships present major difficulties for codependents.

Because of their fears, and because they don't have either good models from their families or personal experience with strong and mutually rewarding relationships, codependent adults don't know what to do to establish or maintain this kind of relationship. They only know about more one-sided arrangements (one of us gives, one of us takes) or of relationships that depend on the more childish levels of coping we described earlier. That is, they bluff, they act helpless, they throw a tantrum, or they leave. Since these people have not yet worked through their deeper fears of abandonment—in fact, they may not even realize that they're scared in this way—their current relationships become distorted by these fears. Distorted relationships, along with our poor skills at working on them, are the major identifying characteristic of codependency, and often are the problem which brings people into treatment or support groups for the first time.

Attempts to Cope

One way we deal with indifference or lack of information about what pleases or displeases others is to take notice of what pleases or displeases ourselves and guess from that. This is called inductive reasoning and is a form of logic that often works pretty well as a rule of thumb. ("If it happened a couple of times, it probably happens a lot." "If I feel this way when that happens, other people probably do too.") This kind of thinking can help a kid figure out a situation, especially when there's little or no information or direction coming from an

adult. Little children assume that their own particular experience sums up the world, and they are amazed to discover later
that not everybody eats supper at five o'clock, not all families
have a dog and two cats, not all daddies have brown eyes, and
so on.

Inductive reasoning has a lot of usefulness but obviously
it's also very limited as a learning tool. Since we're all human,
we do have many shared reactions and common experiences,
but there are also wide variations in situations and details that
cause differences among us. These can break down the value
of inductive conclusions, so that they might not really apply to
the new situation. Maybe we didn't have all the information
we need to base our reasoning on in order to get a reliable conclusion. Maybe the circumstances were a little different this
time from last time, or different for me than they are for you.
With inductive reasoning it can be hard to tell when we have
enough facts to reach a valid conclusion except by trial and
error. This is a pretty risky strategy when the stakes are high,
as they are when we're dealing with issues of abandonment.

So we put a little "body english" on inductive reasoning
to try to make it work better. We may project our beliefs, conclusions or feelings onto other people and act as if they were
the ones who came up with these ideas. We might simply assume that everybody thinks, feels and acts the same way as
ourselves and that if they don't there must be something wrong
with them. We begin to develop inductive reasoning so early
in childhood that we get very good at it and may not even recognize when we're trying to bend the facts to fit our logical
tools, especially if this is the only tool we know how to use.

There is another way to try to cope with the fear of not
being able to please others and therefore ending up alone, and
that is to try to take control of the situation and let the others
worry about pleasing us. Legendary football coach Vince
Lombardi said, "The best defense is a good offense," and some
people seem to adopt this game strategy as a general rule of
life. Frustrated at trying to find out or figure out what the
rules are (or what "normal" is, as Janet Woititz puts it), they
decide to let everybody else catch up with them if not being
alone is so darned important. These people are still making
their decisions with one eye on others to see how they respond,

however. It's a form of the "any-response-is-better-than-no-response-at-all" reaction.

People who adopt this form of coping with fears of being abandoned may try to manipulate or force other people to stay with them. They might try acting helpless or pathetic (who would be so inhuman as to abandon a baby?) or know-it-all (I'm the adult that you need to be near) or angry (you're supposed to stick with me, how dare you leave?) or a combination of any or all of these. They don't believe that anyone will stay with them of their own free will, so they try to stack the deck to guarantee that somebody will be around to take care of them.

Sadly, there are also those people who give up on hoping that others will be there when they need them. They are convinced that they will eventually be abandoned anyway, so they try to lessen the pain of it by being the one who leaves first. They figure that if they can make the abandonment seem like their own choice, it won't be as bad. They're too scared to let anyone get very close for very long because then leaving might hurt anyway, or they might not get the chance to be the one who decides to go. Still, it's hard to give up completely on the hope of having someone there for them, because this hope is so basic to being human. So, these people may ricochet from one relationship to the next, getting intensely involved with someone very quickly as the hope is fresh, then bailing out just as quickly when the "Aha!" experience has gotten familiar and the natural high no longer covers the discomfort of the fear. Kids change "best friends" from week to week at some phases of their development as they work on this issue. Some people get stuck there and don't learn how to keep a relationship going past the infatuation stage, after the newness (and maybe the lust) have worn off.

None of these reactions is sick or even unusual. Each of us uses them during particular stages of normal childhood development and may even fall back on them in specific times and situations as adults. The problem comes if we remain content with these few basic responses to a normal human issue or fear, and don't go on to learn other ways of thinking or coping that are more complex but also work better.

Issue: abandonment
Level: later
Feeling: anxious for acceptance from others
Codependent behaviors: • provoke anger rather than be ignored • handle problems in relationships by bluffs, acting helpless, tantrums, or leaving first • tries to control or manipulate others • gets in and out of relationships quickly

Building Better Skills

One of the most helpful tools for developing better relationship skills is to simply become aware of the fears that are inside us. Once we realize what we are feeling, we have the possibility of choosing when and how to express it to ourselves and to others. We can't choose how to let anyone else in on what's going on inside us unless and until we know what it is ourselves, although the fears may come out on their own in ways in which we might not want them to appear if we do not let ourselves become aware of them. That's the first step in the process—to name some of these feelings and issues so that we can recognize them and begin to deal with them more effectively.

Another helpful tool, once we become aware of a basic fear such as abandonment, is to take stock of the situation instead of letting the discomfort of the fear paralyze us. It's true that a baby is helpless if abandoned, but anyone even a little bit older has a lot more resources than a baby and does not have to be as helpless. Their brains are more fully developed, so that their ability to think is more advanced. They have much more control of their muscles. They know how to speak. People who have been immobilized by the discomfort of the fear may have forgotten that they are no longer as helpless as babies, that they have resources of their own. Physical growth and development alone produce

many more options for us than we started out with as infants;
emotional, social, and mental development add even more.

After we've become aware of ourselves and at least some
of our resources, the time has come to work on our problem-
solving skills. There are many sources to help us develop these
skills, such as educational programs, self-help books, therapy
and support groups. At the core of any constructive method of
working on a problem will be some variation of a process we
could sum up as "observe—judge—act."

Observe: we get as many facts as we can about the problem situation we're in. One set of facts which is often overlooked (but which is extremely important) is how everybody
involved in the situation is feeling. Another important set of
facts that is not always stated is what each person wants from
the outcome of the situation. We also need to take notice of
available resources: from ourselves, other people, social organizations, the surrounding environment and so on.

Judge: when we get the facts together, we start to try to fit
them together in different ways to help generate ideas for a
possible solution. We brainstorm as many choices for working
things out as we can, even if some of them seem silly or im-
practical at the time. If new facts are discovered during this
phase, we factor them in and keep trying to come up with
ideas. Then we take the ideas that we've listed and begin to
weed out the ones which don't fit the problem, whether
because they need resources that we don't have, or they don't
address the feelings and needs of the people involved in the
problem, or they don't fit the available environment, or whatever.

Act: the weeding-out process leaves one or two more-or-
less workable solutions. We choose one and carry it out (even
if it's not perfect) to try to solve the problem. We take careful
notice of how well it works, what about it doesn't work as well
as we'd like, how others react to it, how many resources it uses.
We use these new facts (observe) to decide whether it was a
good solution (judge) and whether we want to use it again in
the future (act).

This process is a form of what our teachers called the scientific method and tried to drum into our heads in grammar
school. It works in dealing with all kinds of human problems,
not just with questions in biology or physics.

In terms of working through fears of being alone, we can use problem-solving skills to take stock of what we're afraid will happen if we are alone, and what we need from the others we want around us. We also can look for other resources that might be available to meet our needs. These would be our *observations*. Then we might consider how we can make use of the resources of family, friends, support groups, churches, service agencies, neighbors and even pets to meet our needs for companionship, affection and intimacy. These would form the basis of our *judgments*. Finally we would try one or more specific ideas to make a series of small changes in our daily lives that might add up to a much larger improvement in the intensity of the fear and its discomfort. These are the *actions* that we take. We can repeat this process as many times as we need or want in order to keep working on the fear.

As we become more skilled and less afraid, we may find that the intensity of our need to be surrounded by others may lessen too. Not that we stop enjoying the company of other people, but that the panic goes out of our desire to socialize. We find ourselves spending time with family or friends because we want to, not because we feel driven to or are afraid not to. We don't feel frantic at the prospect of being alone.

In fact, rather than fearing solitude as a dreaded curse, we may find ourselves actually looking forward to having time alone. We feel less dependent on others to meet our needs or solve our problems because we have taken the time and effort to become aware of our own resources. This means we can risk spending some time by ourselves to explore our own thoughts and interests. We can enjoy a hobby or the library or a museum even if no one is with us.

This time spent alone, once it has been freed from the stranglehold of fear, can become not only pleasant but growthful. We get the opportunity to think, to dream, to create without the distraction of having someone else around. We get the chance to explore ourselves and uncover new aspects of our personalities in much the same way that we get to know another person. This is how we become friends with ourselves. A recent study showed that persons who score high on self-esteem place great value on having time by themselves as well as time with those they love. Both kinds of situations become important to us because we have the freedom to choose either one instead of automatically ruling out the experience of being alone.

Learning to be comfortable with being alone helps us gain many more choices. Our activities don't have to be restricted by the availability of someone to come along with us or by our ability to convince someone to stay. We can relax and enjoy other people's company, because our fear of their leaving is not competing for our attention at the same time—or at least has quieted somewhat. We know that we are not still helpless babies and that we have resources. We may not know everything, but we know how to solve problems and how to ask for help when we need it. We are never truly alone because we've got ourselves to fall back on. We still value others and want to be with them, but it's okay to be alone too. We have the freedom to choose.

Issue: abandonment
Level: adult
Feelings: loving and being loved
Target behaviors: • awareness of the fears and needs we have about others • take stock of resources to keep from being helpless or alone • observe—judge—act • learning to enjoy the times when we're alone

This is a tragic story, a story of a woman and a man who could not get their relationship together.

She was a wealthy woman at the time she met him. She lived in one of those little Mediterranean countries that are famous for their shipping and commerce, and her father had given her to a rich old man as a wife when she was just a young girl. Despite this, she had loved her husband, and she was devastated when he died. Some time after her husband's death, she learned that her jealous, greedy brother had arranged to have him murdered—but she had no proof. Eventually, she stole a huge amount of her brother's money and fled the country. He did not dare come after her for fear his crime would be discovered. She landed in another little country in that part of the world and bought a large area of land where, for all intents and purposes, her word became law. An adult child made good.

One day she met a newcomer to her land. He was a general, unfortunately on the losing side of a civil war from yet another little Mediterranean country. He had been a lateral member of the royal family which was now deposed. He had escaped in the final hours of the very last battle. He had had to argue his aged father into leaving the country along with him and his wife and son. In the confusion of their escape, his wife was lost, never to be seen alive again. He and a small band of followers ricocheted through the islands and countries thereabouts, and eventually ended up in the city where she was now living.

At first she just extended the courtesy one would expect to give a rich, handsome professional man, but soon she was swept off her feet by him. They had a mad, passionate affair for months which made both their names household words. She doted on his son from his first marriage; they spent all day every day together doing all those lifestyles-of-the-rich-and-famous things. She was deliriously happy and thought he was too.

Meanwhile, he began to feel guilty about abandoning the cause of restoring a homeland for his people, and about betraying his son's future. Without letting her know, he began to make plans to leave the country. Well, of course she found out about his plans, and they had a huge fight. She accused him of trying to leave without even saying goodbye; he accused her of putting promises in his mouth that he had never made. The argument got louder and more heated, until she roundly cursed him and wished him dead, and he left her house.

Later, however, she had a change of heart and tried to make up with him. She tried to get him to agree to stay just a little longer and then she wouldn't try to make him stay forever. But he would not even send her a reply. She put up a good front about accepting this outcome, and even watched him leave the city. Then she sent her sister and her maid away on a pretext and committed a rather messy suicide by stabbing herself after setting fire to her bedroom. Her lover didn't hear of her death until much later, and when he did he expressed some regret but did not attempt to contact anyone from her family. Eventually he did set up a new homeland for his people. He took a local woman as his second wife, although he never loved her the way he had loved either his first wife or his rich, adoring mistress.

This is not a 20th century story which inquiring minds want to know. It is not a fairy tale. It is the story of Aeneas, the legendary founder of Rome in 753 B.C., and of Dido, a queen of Libya, as retold by Publius Virgilius Maro (19 B.C.). Codependency has been around for a long, long time.

Related Readings

Halpern, Howard M., *How to Break Your Addiction to a Person,* New York: McGraw-Hill, 1982.

Hendrix, Harville, *Getting the Love You Want,* New York: Henry Holt and Company, Inc., 1988.

Mumey, Jack, *Loving An Alcoholic,* Chicago: Contemporary Books, Inc., 1985.

Restak, Richard M., *The Brain,* New York: Bantam Books, 1984.

— 3 —

What Do You Think?
(And How Do You Know?)

"Once upon a time. . . ." The surest way to get an attentive audience is to begin a story with these words. Everyone knows that a tale set in once-upon-a-time will be filled with magic and mythical beasts and warriors and princesses, and not be limited by the boundaries of ordinary rules or logic. We never get too old to stop and listen to a story like this. We don't care if it's not filled with historical or scientific truths—in fact, that's one of the main reasons we're interested. We want to be amazed and charmed and frightened and entertained. We want to go back to a time we never knew.

Or did we? We may not have run into any wizards or castles recently, but we all pass through a time in our lives when things seem to happen by magical processes we don't understand. In fact, much of our lives is spent trying to get enough knowledge and skill to master our surroundings and ourselves, to understand the mysterious ways things work.

Young children experience most of their reality as somewhat magical. Their attention is very limited in terms of time and scope, so they can usually focus only for short bursts and on only a small part of a process or an idea at any given time. They experience life as a series of loosely connected activities and ideas. They accept that various things happen—it's dark when I go to bed and light when I get up; the refrigerator is cold inside; oranges taste sweet and lemons don't—but they don't understand how or why.

There are a number of factors that help explain this "magical thinking," most of which have to do with the fact that human babies are born at such an early stage of physical development. Babies' brains and nervous systems are not fully developed at birth. The nerves and the pathways for nerve impulses continue to develop for years afterward, in part with the help of the stimulation from the sights and sounds and events around us. Certain kinds of thought processes just aren't possible until the brain has developed enough of the right kinds of connections in the proper places. Research in brain chemistry and development is very exciting in what we're finding out about how our basic brain equipment combines with our experiences of the people and things in our environment to develop our many capabilities for thought, understanding, memory, creativity, body management, learning, and self-expression.

Brain development in a newborn baby is amazingly complex compared to where it began nine months earlier, but it's simple and incomplete compared to the level it can eventually achieve (as long as nothing goes wrong or is injured). A newborn's brain can already direct her automatic life processes: breathing, digestion, blood circulation, eliminating body wastes, and the five senses. It has some beginning capabilities for directing voluntary movements such as sucking, turning the head, moving arms and legs, closing the fist, and crying. It works constantly at improving its control of voluntary movements because this kind of control is what the baby needs to develop in order to survive. So many of the accomplishments of a baby's first year are physical ones—holding the head up, focusing the eyes, grabbing an object and bringing it to the mouth, rolling over, crawling, sitting up, standing, walking. These occur in the same general order for most babies because their brains are growing and developing in the same general order or sequence.

Babies learn to react to and interact with their surroundings too, especially with the people around them. This is, of course, also a matter of survival for a helpless infant. Babies show an inborn preference for looking at faces even when other interesting things are available to look at. Their eyes first begin to focus at a distance of about 8 - 10 inches from their faces, just about where the face of the person who is nursing or feeding them would be. Within a few weeks after birth they learn to return a smile. They coo when others speak softly to them, then learn to make sounds to try to prompt a response from others.

They learn to recognize a familiar face and to show a preference for family members over strangers.

We use this natural interest in and preference for people,
especially for family members as the baby learns to recognize
them, as a reward and a motivator in the process of helping the
baby learn the skills to master his or her body. We hold the
rattle near our own face and shake it gently to help the child
direct his attention to focus on the rattle so that he can try to
grab it. We take a few steps back and hold out our arms as we
encourage the baby to "come to Mommy." We repeat the same
simple words over and over to help the baby learn to pro-
nounce them. And we give lots of smiles and hugs and kisses
for each effort—as well as for no other reason besides our affection for the baby.

A baby's development is focused on survival and the
growth necessary for that. Their brains develop the ability to
control ever more specialized groups of muscles to help the
baby achieve this growth. For example, first the baby can flail
her arms and grab whatever happens to be placed within her
fist; then she learns to control her arm enough to move it toward a toy, then to grab the toy in a fist, and eventually to use
finger and thumb to pick up even smaller objects. While babies
are developing these skills they are also beginning to develop
memory and learning. They are laying the foundations for
more complex thought processes which will develop after survival skills have had time to be learned.

Research on these patterns of development for thought
processes has been conducted by many scientists. While some
theories differ on certain points, there seems to be general
agreement on the order in which we learn how to think: first
we try to make sense of the outside world, then we focus on
more internal kinds of processes.

Earliest Types of Thinking

Since babies and young children use their brains mostly to
learn the skills to gain control of their bodies and of their physical surroundings, it is no surprise that the evidence we have of
their thought processes shows that their thinking is guided by
images and patterns based on experience with movement and
information from the five senses. That is, when children begin

talking well enough to make themselves understood, the way they do this suggests that they are thinking in much the same way that they experienced their world in the first place: lots of specific details, focused on concrete objects, colored by their emotions and reactions to the event without knowing that the feelings were inside them while the event happened outside them.

Babies and small children don't have a sense of a "boundary" between their inner reactions and outside reality. If they are hungry, tired, or in pain, they cry; they don't have to think about it, they just react. If they want something, they expect it to appear in much the same way that Mommy seemed to appear with food when they cried as infants, simply because they know that they want it. A stimulus from the outside world provokes an immediate response from the child, and at this stage of development it will almost certainly be in the form of physical movement of some kind. Any thinking that the child does is focused on the sense information that he spends so much time and energy gathering.

This is one reason why kids are so impulsive and easily distractable. From the moment of birth onwards, we are constantly being bombarded with information about sights, sounds, textures, smells, and tastes from the world around us. We quickly learn to tune out extra stimulation in order to focus on the most important cues for getting what we want or need. T. Berry Brazelton, a nationally known pediatrician and author, has noted that newborns show the ability to ignore loud noises after the first time they hear them while they are still in the delivery room! A new sound or other new stimulus, though, claims our attention for the first time or two because we need to find out whether it is important or not, to see if it will affect us directly. (For example, the baby wants to know: does this person pick me up? Feed me? Make noises? Do I start to feel pain? Does this feel good?) Most experiences of the outside world are pretty new to babies and small children, so they have to pay attention to more of them in order to figure out whether they're important. Kids can't stand it if they think they might be missing something, so they have trouble screening out distractions in order to focus on only the matter at hand. This is a normal, helpful part of human development.

It also results in the easy distractability of small children, which is both a blessing and a curse. Little kids are usually easy to distract and comfort when they are distressed because we can get them interested in some other stimulus in the immediate surroundings. ("Oh, look at that doggie!") Their thinking is focused on immediate sense or movement information, and their brains are not yet developed to the point that they can keep on thinking about something unless they have a reminder available through their senses to keep their attention focused on it. Other new and interesting information crowds out the original thought unless it has very great meaning or urgency.

On the other hand, if children return to a sight, a smell, a location where they experienced something, they can often recall other sense information associated with that event in clear detail much more readily than can an adult who might have been there too. The adult will just see the neighborhood street that they always pass on the way to the library; the toddler will say "Choo-choo train?" as she gets to the spot where they were on their last outing when the train whistle blew, even if it has been a week or more since then. Train whistles are ho-hum to the adult but fascinating to the child, and as she re-experiences some of the same sense data from the surroundings, it prompts the additional memory of the whistle she heard. Meanwhile, her parent is trying to figure out what she means, because he doesn't remember the minor (to him) detail of the whistle.

The ready availability of interesting sense and movement stimulation for children also feeds their natural impulsiveness. For a kid, to think is to act. They do not yet have either the experience or the ability to be able to stop and consider the consequences of an activity they may have thought of. "Just do it" is an expression of this level of thinking. They may be able to plan ahead enough to gather some of the things they will need in order to carry out whatever project has entered their heads, but they are not likely to be able to stop and focus enough to judge what the results will be, either physically (will I get hurt?) or morally (will I get into trouble?). They will get started on one project, see something that distracts them to a new line of thought and abandon the first plan without so much as a backward glance. Actions follow sense or movement stimulation on the spur of the moment, with very little thought coming between getting the impulse and carrying it out.

This also means that it's difficult for young children to plan ahead or to imagine a future event unless they have already experienced something like it before, because they process information based on what they have learned with their senses or their ability to move. They need to have new ideas or events explained in familiar terms and tied to people, places or activities which they already know. Their ability to think ahead is very limited; they need guidance from adults or older children in order to consider "what happens next" in an unfamiliar situation.

So, much of a small child's daily experience has a sort of magical quality to it. They really aren't sure just how events are related, and therefore almost everything carries a faint air of wonder and amazement at least the first few times. A five-year-old will place her fingertip over the place where her coloring went outside the lines in the coloring book, then check to see if the mistake disappeared. A four-year-old will answer a question that Big Bird asked on TV and be sure that Big Bird heard him. Young children take their experiences, and the explanations that we adults give in answer to their questions, pretty much at face value. They don't yet have the mental capability to analyze concepts that are not based on direct experience. They learn by doing, and try many things over and over and over again as they struggle to predict what the outcome will be. A different outcome seems like magic—that's the only way a small child can make sense of it.

For example, a preschooler who is singing his ABC's has to start all over again from the beginning if he is interrupted or forgets a letter in the middle. He learned the song in a particular order, and if that order is disturbed he doesn't yet know how to rearrange the parts and just pick up from where he left off. He can only process the information in the same way he experienced it the first time. As he grows older and his brain capability expands, he will learn how to separate the parts of the song and sing whatever part he wants without having to run through the whole song to get there. But for now, his ability to think is limited by his brain's need to function at a level which focuses development on senses-movement learning and (in the early school-age years) on the transition to cause-and-effect thinking. He will need lots of practice and instruction from grown-ups or older children in order to progress to the next levels of thinking processes. Adult children and other codependents may not have received this kind of instruction in a reliable way during their early years if the adults in their families were busy with their own problems and not available for this sort of communication. As a result, they may continue to think primarily in this impulsive, random way of recalling, and possibly being distracted by, impressions gathered from their senses as well as their own internal reactions to their surroundings.

Of course we do not lose this ability to think in concrete terms when we move ahead in our cognitive (mental) development. We always maintain the ability, if our brains have not been sedated or injured, to remember events in chronological order, to notice details of color, aroma, texture, or sensation; it's "just like riding a bicycle" and has some things in common with this kind of muscle-memory. Some of us can get stuck at this early level of development, however, in the sense that we continue to use this as a primary way of processing information or ideas. It's not a bad way to think, but it is very limited, and limiting in terms of the kinds of conversations we can have and the types of problems we feel equipped to deal with.

Adults who are using this mode of thinking as their primary method have trouble summarizing an experience, or picking out the highlights, or realizing what they learned from it. When they get home from work they have to give a blow-by-blow account of what happened to them during the day, giving great detail about conversations, activities, reactions to events, even private thoughts and opinions. They can describe something so well that their listeners almost feel as if they had been there too, but then may forget to mention why this event was important (and may not in fact have a clear sense of why it is important themselves, either). If they are interrupted, they may need to repeat some of what they already said in order to get back into the flow of what they were saying. They may also repeat the same story several times in much the same way over a period of time, more as a means to help their memory or understanding than as a way to communicate it clearly to someone else.

Another related characteristic of codependent behavior at this stage of development is poor planning skills and an inability to foresee the consequences of a course of action ahead of time. That is, some codependents tend to find themselves in the midst of a (problem) situation without the slightest notion of either how they got into it or how they can get out of it. They follow the impulse to "just do it" and then have to spend much more effort getting themselves out of the jam which that impulse created than they would have had to spend in thinking things through in the first place—if only they had thought of doing just that. This is thinking at an early level of development which does not take advantage of more advanced kinds of thought processes that become possible as our brains continue to grow. It's familiar and comfortable, and an entirely normal kind of thinking; however, it will be grossly inadequate after we get beyond early childhood and start to face the kinds of situations that adults face.

It may be within this early level of thinking that denial begins too. Denial is a very basic form of human response to bad news or uncomfortable situations. Our automatic response when something bad happens—"Oh, no! That can't be!"—is a protective measure which allows us, at its best, to buy ourselves a few seconds or minutes to absorb the bad news so that we can decide how to deal with it. This temporary denial of reality, in which we just X-out the unwelcome parts of our world, may have its beginnings in the experiences of early childhood when much of life seemed to be unconnected and open to challenge by mysterious forces.

We certainly develop the ability to deny what we don't like early in life; two-year-olds are famous for being able to express "No!" very clearly and firmly when faced with an unwanted limit, and the ability to refuse to deal with painful realities can be seen even earlier in some instances. Denial is helpful only when it is used as a *temporary* tool to help us gather our resources for dealing with a problem, however. The problems which arise when chemically dependent or codependent people use denial as a means of consistently avoiding realities which they would rather not face are many, complicated, and well-known. Basically, denying a problem for more than a few moments tends only to make it worse. This is a twisting of the natural developmental step of saying "no" to things we as small children did not understand or feel equipped to deal with. A little kid says "no" and hopes that this will take care of things. An adult knows that problems rarely disappear on their own, and that the only way to have any hope of getting the result to go the way we want is to deal with the problem directly ourselves.

Issue: kinds of thinking processes
Level: earliest
Thinking: information from senses, movement
Codependent behaviors: • easily distracted • random thoughts strung together • heavy on details • can't plan ahead or see consequences • overuse of denial

The Beginnings of Logical Thought

If children continue to develop in the normal sequence of thinking and learning, they move beyond this preoccupation with sense data and ways of dealing with it to more internal, logical forms of thought. Children begin to develop a sense of how various parts of their surroundings or parts of an event relate to each other, and can begin to grasp more of the aspects of a situation all at once instead of having to focus on only a small part of it at a time. The first steps in this direction are a far cry from fully adult patterns of thinking, though, and are still heavily influenced by concrete experiences with people and objects.

This kind of thinking begins with a "what happens next" approach which builds on the child's memories of previous experiences. As the child's brain continues to develop, he or she can now begin to reason about what *might* happen next, again based on past experiences under a number of different circumstances. Rather than having to simply reproduce an experience exactly the way it happened the first time, kids can begin to recognize patterns from a number of activities and to attempt to use this information as a guide or rule for dealing with new but similar circumstances. In other words, they are learning how to figure something out without having to act it out. They are beginning to learn how to use reason and logic, not just to process incoming sense information.

One of the first indications that this shift in thinking processes is starting is the ability to understand cause and effect: if I do this, then that will happen. Children begin to look for common characteristics in their experiences with a particular toy or person or situation so that they can start to predict what will happen when they encounter it again:

"When I drop the egg on the floor, it cracks."

"If I color on Daddy's papers, he gets mad."

"After I get hot and sweaty playing outside, I need a cool drink."

They begin to group certain kinds of actions or experiences together in order to figure out the common rule or outcome, and eventually move from this kind of analysis-after-the-fact to trying to predict what will happen next time.

Even after this shift has begun to occur, kids still put their experiences into little separate mental boxes quite a bit. They can be happily convinced that ideas which contradict each other are still both true, because they have applied them to different situations—or else because they simply refuse to see the contradiction.

For example, bad guys are mean and good guys are nice; kids have no trouble identifying who is who in a cartoon or movie. Kids can also label other children whom they know only slightly as being "good" or "bad" and will offer examples of the child's behavior to justify giving this label. People whom the child knows better and has a continuing personal relationship with, however, tend to be defined as "good" even though they may at times act in a way which angers or scares the child and thus is "not nice." The child either switches back and forth between the good-guy and bad-guy labels, or ignores the mean behavior in assigning the good-guy label. The contradiction itself is not recognized or dealt with as yet.

As kids grow and develop, however, this kind of compartmentalized thinking begins to give way to the realization that there are patterns in their experience with objects and people, and that these experiences or people can be grouped together according to these patterns. Kids can begin to classify information according to these patterns and to use their knowledge to think about entirely new situations which they have never experienced. This is the beginning of what we call formal or logical thought.

This step depends on the child learning to think in abstract terms; that is, the child must learn to separate one special aspect of a specific object or person or situation to think about, without losing sight of the wholeness of the object. The child learns to think in terms of what scientists call variables (color, weight, size, volume, elasticity, etc.) and to consider these characteristics of the object separately in order to learn more about the object as a whole. This leads to the possibility of refining the "if-then" thinking processes to one which keeps all other conditions the same except the single variable the child wants to explore, and then changing around just that one characteristic. This is the basis for doing scientific experiments, which kids at this stage of development get very interested in.

As this type of thinking develops, kids learn to combine the groupings or classes of objects or experiences which they have begun to construct into larger classes of classes. Their ability to use abstract thought improves, so that they don't need to use only concrete experience as a basis for their thinking, but can reason from verbal statements about their environment instead. Rather than having to test the statement that the stove is hot (as a younger child who has not reached this stage of development would), the child can accept that statement and draw the conclusion that he'd better not leave the ice cubes on it because they'll melt.

Before a kid reaches the stage of logical thought, she reasons only from particular situations to a general truth. This is *inductive* reasoning, and it is a valuable tool. The development of logical thought permits the additional tool of *deductive* reasoning, or using a general rule to understand a new situation. The key word here is *understand*; kids can memorize and apply general rules before this stage, but they will not really be able to make sense of the rule on their own. That's why younger children who have not yet truly developed logical thought capabilities are forever getting into trouble, because they tried to apply a rule they have already learned in a situation where it doesn't fit. When the rule doesn't work, they don't have the slightest idea why it didn't and have no way to figure out what would have to change in order for the rule to apply. They cannot use deductive reasoning because they haven't developed the "brain power" for it yet.

This is a stage of development where adult children often are struggling. They may not have had enough instruction or practice in order to sharpen their skills at abstract thinking, so that deductions of how to apply a general rule to a new specific situation simply escape them. They try to memorize the rules so that they can get along with others, but since they grew up in a system where the rules were erratic and not very dependable, they haven't learned how to come up with a rule that is general enough to be applied successfully to new or different situations. They are not stupid by any means, but they have not had the opportunity to sharpen their skills to their full potential.

Codependent adults who are stuck in this stage of development may find themselves having experiences like the young man in one of Grimm's fairy tales:

Jack went to town and bought a needle for his mother. He stuck the needle in a haywagon on his way home and lost it. His mother scolded him and told him he should have stuck it in his sleeve for safekeeping. Jack apologized and said he'd try to remember that. The next day Jack went to town and bought a knife. He stuck it in his sleeve to bring home and on the way it slid out and was lost. His mother scolded him and said he should have put it in his pocket. Jack again apologized and said he'd try to remember that. In the same way, Jack tried to bring home a goat in his pocket; a ham by leading it home on a string; a calf by wrapping it in paper and carrying it in his arms; and a young lady by tying a rope around her neck and fastening her to the manger!

Poor Jack could remember the rules but could not understand their logic, and so failed again and again in spite of good intentions and honest effort. He had not yet developed the skill of thinking logically.

Research on the human brain indicates that the ability to think logically has a great deal to do with a person's ability to use language. For most people, the ability to process language is centered primarily in the left half of their brains, and it is

Issue: kinds of thinking processes
Level: middle
Thinking: • "what happens next"   • cause and effect   • inductive reasoning
Codependent behaviors: • memorize "rules" but don't really understand their reasoning   • see things only from my own viewpoint

from this circumstance that we have gotten used to referring to left-brain-influenced thinking as logical or rational.

Many experiments have been done with people who have had the connecting nerve pathways between the right sides and the left sides of their brains cut as a last-ditch means to control seizures which would not respond to medication. Cutting the pathways does not affect these people's ability to lead normal lives; in fact, most of us would not be able to tell any difference in how the person usually acts even after the pathways have been cut. What this procedure does is to prevent the two sides of the person's brain from communicating directly with each other in the way a normal brain can; this has led to some interesting experiments which have helped scientists learn a lot about how our brains work.

We know that, generally speaking, the right side of the brain controls the left side of the body and the left side of the brain controls the right side of the body. A series of experiments which build on this fact were set up so that the person in the experiment ended up having to explain why he had chosen pictures with each hand from a lineup of choices in front of him. The experimenters knew that the person's right hand had chosen a picture that matched the information which the left side of his brain had seen, and that his left hand had chosen a picture to match the different information given to the right side of his brain. The person himself didn't know that the two halves of his brain had received different information because the pathways that ordinarily would have allowed the two sides of the brain to "compare notes" had been cut. In addition, the person couldn't say directly why the right half of his brain had chosen the picture with his left hand, because his ability to speak (use language) is controlled by the left side of his brain, and the left side didn't know the reason for the right side's choice. How the person handled this situation of having to explain a choice when he wasn't able to put the reason into words has some strong implications for all of us.

Time after time, the person would easily identify why he had chosen the picture controlled by the left side of his brain (the side that processes language), and then he would come up with some outlandish but logical reason for having chosen the other picture too. The person would not hesitate, or indicate that he was guessing, or show any kind of uncertainty about the reason for his other hand's choice—even though, as the experimenters knew, the left side of his brain was making it up, since it didn't have the information that the right side of the brain did. The reason which the person's left brain gave was always wrong (that is, it didn't match the information that the right brain had received as a basis for choosing the picture), but it was always offered as a statement of fact, not as a guess. The logical processes just took over full responsibility for making sense of the situation, even though the necessary information was not available. Both men and women would respond in this same way to this experiment, time after time.

This kind of experiment may shed some light on a common characteristic of adult children: their ability to rationalize or explain away behavior which is destructive to themselves or to their relationships. They honestly may not know why they take back their abusive lover, or gorge on unwanted food, or clean up after their chemically dependent child; or perhaps they may know deep down in their hearts the reason for this kind of response, but may be denying it to themselves. Either way, the necessary information is not available to their logical selves, but that doesn't stop them from concocting an apparently logical reason to justify the destructive behavior. The combination of denial and rationalization makes possible the elaborate system of lies which support and enable codependent and chemically dependent behavior. We can make up rational reasons for almost any of our actions—never mind that these have absolutely nothing to do with the real reasons why we do things. And once we've come up with these logical reasons, we will sincerely defend them to the end as if they were true, because they seem true to our logical selves. It is only after all the information is presented (after we "face facts" or "hit bottom" or otherwise allow all of our conscious self to see all of the situation) that the part of us that thinks logically can stop rationalizing and accept the truth, then start to decide what to do about it.

Once a person develops the capability for logical thought, other possibilities for new perspectives open up. The ability to focus on a particular variable and consider it apart from others in the environment leads to the possibility of thinking about one's own self and experiences. A self-awareness of one's habits or characteristics emerges from this process. Kids begin to become aware of and able to name their feelings; this allows them to be able to reflect on the feeling and consider how to express it or deal with it during quiet times when they are not in the grips of the emotion, instead of just reacting out of their guts on the spur of the moment as smaller kids do.

Another possibility which opens up in this stage of development is the ability to look at a situation from someone else's viewpoint instead of only my own. Small children are not able to understand that other people see things differently from themselves, whether in a physical sense (if I'm facing in a different direction I can't see the same scene in the same way that you do) or on a more abstract level. Six-year-old Susie is quite sure that Mom would love a dollhouse for her birthday because Susie would like one herself, and she doesn't understand that Mom might have a different perspective on dollhouses. In a few years when Susie has matured a little more, she will be able to develop an awareness of Mom's preferences even when these do not coincide with her own.

This ability to see a situation from another person's point of view is the foundation for true *empathy:* the ability to understand what someone else is feeling without necessarily feeling that same way yourself. This skill broadens our horizons emotionally in much the same way that understanding someone else's ideas expands our mental capabilities. These capacities help us to see what we have in common with others, and allow us to expand our worldviews to include others beyond just ourselves or our immediate families.

The emergence of these skills is not automatic, however. The readiness which sets the stage for their appearance is a result of the growth and maturation of our brains, but the actual development of the skill takes time, effort, and opportunity. We have to be taught how to apply the skills which our brains are ready to acquire. Just because it's now possible for me to figure out how to conduct an experiment or to see the merits of an opposite opinion, doesn't mean that I have actually tried it. And even when I do try it, I will need practice and repetition in order to get good at it, just like any other skill. I will make mistakes along the way, and I will have to deal with the consequences of those mistakes.

This may be what keeps many codependent adults from having mastered the skills of logical thought. The families in which they grew up, as well as many of the people in their adult lives, may not have allowed the necessary practice and mistake-making which we must go through in order to get good at thinking logically. The stakes for not being right or not being perfect are just too high for these people, so they prefer to go with what they know, which pretty much leaves them stuck with concrete thinking processes. They cannot bear the threat of disapproval or abandonment which hangs over every mistake, so they can't or won't take the chance to practice their more abstract thought processes. Besides, they may have fewer models to teach them how to do abstract thinking if they are in relationship systems with others who are equally stuck in earlier thought patterns. It's hard to teach someone what you don't know yourself.

Issue: kinds of thinking processes
Level: later
Thinking: • logic • abstract thought • deductive reasoning
Codependent behaviors: • rationalization • needing to be "right," not mistaken

Beyond Formal Thought

Some authors suggest that there are thought processes even beyond the ability to think logically. They feel that the ability to think about abstract characteristics grows into a capacity to think in terms of systems, and to see how we as individuals fit into these systems. A person becomes able not only to reflect on herself as an individual but also to see how her environment (including relationships) affects her and others. This is the stage in which we integrate what we know about ourselves with what we know about other persons, objects and situations. Putting all these viewpoints together helps us decide whether we want to make any changes in our lives or our surroundings, and how to go about doing that.

It is within this stage of thinking that questions of meaning become particularly important. Concrete objects don't have too much uncertainty about their meaning: either they're there or they aren't. Logical thinking begins to raise the question of meaning because we are beginning to manipulate objects and their characteristics solely within our minds, and the decision of which characteristics to consider and which to ignore says that we have assigned some value or meaning to them in order to choose. When we consider systems and their effect on us, we are dealing almost exclusively with abstractions, and the patterns we decide to consider are chosen on the basis of our understanding of their consequences for us and for others. The understanding or meaning we assign to these systems often then colors how we view the events in our lives themselves. (For example, I might accept being called a "dumb Polack" by another person of Polish descent without being offended by it, but be very angry if a supervisor at work called me that in a public meeting.)

People who are able to think in terms of systems ask themselves questions about how they can integrate, or put together, the various happenings in their lives so that they can learn something from them. They are trying to get a sense of themselves as a consistent personality rather than being content just to notice various recurring patterns of behavior in themselves. They work on being able to identify and talk about themselves with a real sense of self instead of as a walking bundle of contradictions. They try to become aware of how they got to be who they are: what forces in their families, schools, neighborhood, circle of friends, jobs, church, clubs, or society helped to shape the person they see themselves to be. At the same time, they look at how they may have contributed to those systems and how they may have had an impact on influencing themselves and others.

It is very rare to see this type of thought process in anyone who is not at least in young adulthood, and many people never develop this ability at all. Someone who has learned to think in systemic terms has the ability to use both inductive and deductive reasoning and to move back and forth between them, both to form general rules about their experiences and to apply those rules to new situations—or to apply them to previous experiences in order to understand them in a new way. A person like this would not only ask herself how she has been affected by racism, for example, but would start to be able to think about how she has acted in a racist way herself in different situations and how she might avoid doing so in the future. This probably would not be a particularly comfortable exercise for her to do, but at least it would be possible. On the other hand, the whole topic might never even occur to those who have not developed the skill of thinking in terms of systems— or if it did come up for some reason, they would not know how to get the mental distance from their various experiences to be able to think it through. These people therefore would never get the chance to work on shaping the larger situations of their lives, but have to be content with just reacting to events without ever having a very clear notion of how they themselves fit into the bigger picture.

Only someone who has learned to take a look at systems and their own place in them is able to think about changing the systems and to work on strategies for how to do that. Just as a person who has learned how to think logically can "step outside" himself in order to become aware of himself as a person separate from his environment, a person who thinks systemically can step outside his systems and look at them in a more objective way. He no longer accepts them as "just the way things are" and can begin to consider whether the way things are is good enough. He begins to question meanings which up till now he has always just assumed or taken for granted:

- What if families don't automatically offer assistance to someone who insists on screwing up?
- What if a person can get affection without having to act helpless?
- How can people show love to others without going along with or cleaning up after self-destructive acts?

The struggle for answers to this type of question has the potential not only to change this person's life, but to transform his entire system as well. He will have to think in terms of putting together ideas which appear to contradict each other, and will have to consider outlooks wider than just his own experience or the experience of those he knows personally in order to do this. It's not as easy as just mentally moving concrete experiences around, but it can be much more satisfying and have far greater impact on his life.

Issue: kinds of thinking process
Level: adult
Thinking: systems
Target behaviors: • seeing how I fit into larger systems • expanding values and meanings • seeing myself as a whole person

As we said, even people who would not consider themselves codependent may not develop the skills of this stage of thinking or cognitive process. The fact that we can identify these skills, though, lets us know that this type of wisdom is possible and is something we can strive for as we master the skills of the previous stages.

Building Better Skills

So how do we sharpen our thinking skills to take full advantage of the capabilities which we can develop as adults?

We start with an awareness of what the possibilities are in our-selves and an assessment of what skills we are currently using.

The temptation is to try to jump ahead in our development and acquire late-stage skills as fast as we can. Unfortunately, this just isn't possible, as far as we can tell. All the research on stages of development indicates that we must pass through the stages in the same sequence as they have been discussed here as we mature. Nobody can skip a step and maybe go back and pick it up later. We have to experience each kind of thinking process in order to prepare ourselves for the next.

If we are already adults when we begin to concentrate on furthering our cognitive (mental) development, however, we won't necessarily have to spend as long a time in each task as a child would. Children seem to have to wait until their brains have matured enough before they can go on in their develop-ment. Adults, having reached the point of mature physical growth, have the readiness to progress onto the next level with-out having to wait for their bodies to catch up. Therefore, no matter where I locate myself among the various stages of cogni-tive development, I can make an effort to practice all the skills of that level so that I get a thorough basis for stretching my wings and moving ahead to a more advanced kind of thinking, as quickly as I can.

We never lose the skills of the previous levels as we grow, and they have real usefulness even in later life. We need to be able to tune into random sense impressions at times in order to jog our memories for some important but forgotten detail, or to come up with a concrete solution to a concrete problem. These are important skills and they deserve to be maintained. We just need to make sure that as we face more complex situations as adults, we also develop the very best mental tools we can for dealing with those situations. For most of us, that will mean at least some of the skills of logical thought so that we can ana-lyze situations or relationships in order to see how we might improve them.

A particularly important logical skill for this is the ability to take a look at myself in as objective a manner as I can: "to see ourselves as others see us," as poet Robert Burns said. Peo-ple who score high on intelligence tests have been found to be people who talk to themselves as they try to figure out a task or a situation. Maybe talking to yourself isn't always the "crazy" behavior we've all feared that it might be; maybe sometimes it's a reflection of the ability to take a step back from what you're doing in order to observe and judge it the way you might do so with someone else.

A related skill to foster in ourselves as we mature is a sense of humor. There are various levels of humor, ranging from slapstick and pratfalls through puns and jokes all the way up to sophisticated stories which refer to specialized subjects. Most of the higher forms of humor that we call wit, however, depend on the ability to stand outside oneself or one's situation and take a detached, fresh look at it. There is growing evidence that a sense of humor helps those who are sick to hasten and expand their bodies' powers of healing. It may be that a sense of humor can also assist in extending our growth and development.

At least, the possibilities for growth are there if we are using humor as a tool for increasing our understanding, rather than as a defense against letting someone get close to us or as a weapon for attack. We can tell the difference between these various uses of humor by noting the results.

- Does my use or enjoyment of this joke expand my understanding of this situation?

- Does it help me get closer to the ones I care about in a meaningful way?

- Does it help me work through an uncomfortable situation to make it better, instead of just abandoning the mess or perhaps even making the problem worse?

Yes answers to questions like these indicate a growthful use of wit and humor.

The skills that we acquire as we make progress in logical thought processes can also become distorted, particularly as they combine with our feelings. For example, our ability to analyze a situation for problems can combine with our dread of making a mistake and possibly being abandoned, so that we start imagining disasters behind every little glitch and become too paralyzed by fear to act at all. Or we may get so used to classifying things in our surroundings into groups and labeling them, that we forget to consider the special uniqueness of each thing because we stopped with the label. We can get around these distortions, but only if we watch for them in ourselves and use our thinking skills along with an awareness of our feelings and fears to get ourselves back on track. There is a type of therapy called cognitive or rational-emotive which specializes in helping people do just that. The principles can be learned from books or with a therapist.

We never really get back to "once upon a time," no matter how many stories we listen to. If we make the most of our thinking abilities as we develop, however, we can appreciate the childlike qualities of that time without paying the price of getting stuck in childish illogic. That may lead us to the very best time of all.

An elephant chanced near a village in India, and six old men who had been blind from birth were led out to the place where the elephant was so that they could examine it.

The first man happened to grasp the elephant's trunk as he came near. He felt the length and suppleness of it, and noticed the ease and grace of its movement. "Aha!" thought the old man. "An elephant is very like a snake."

The second man, who had walked at the side of the first, felt the strong, smooth tusk beneath his hands. He followed its tapering shape down to the point. "Aha!" he decided. "An elephant is much like a spear."

The third man, who had walked alongside the other two, was smacked in the face by the elephant's ear. He caught it and gently explored its thin membranes, and the way it stirred the air. "Aha!" he concluded. "An elephant is very similar to a fan."

The fourth man, an adventurous sort, walked straight up to the elephant and ran right into its side. He reached out to catch himself and felt the broad, flat surface of its huge body. The elephant was hardly aware of the man's small brown form and barely moved. "Aha!" said the old man to himself. "An elephant bears a strong resemblance to a wall."

The fifth old man was a little unsteady on his feet, and stumbled just as he reached the elephant. As he groped for a way to get up, his hand touched the elephant's leg. He felt its sturdy strength and wrinkled texture. "Aha! An elephant is distinctly like a tree."

The sixth old man wandered a bit and might have missed the elephant entirely, when the beast flicked at some flies and landed its tail in the man's hand. The old man easily explored its thin flexibility and bristly end. "Aha!" he knew, "an elephant is nearly the same as a rope."

The men were returned to their village, where they began to compare their observations. A heated argument broke out and continued long into that night, and the next, and the next. Each man insisted on the truth of his own experience and denied any worth to the others'. As it was, each one was partly right, but since each insisted on listening only to himself, all of them ended up mistaken.

Related Readings

Brazelton, T. Berry, *Infants and Mothers: Differences in Development*, New York: Dell Publishing Company, Inc., 1969.

Burns, David, *Feeling Good: The New Mood Therapy*, New York: William Morrow and Company, Inc., 1980.

Richmond, P. G., *An Introduction to Piaget*, New York: Basic Books, Inc., 1971.

Springer, Sally P., and Deutsch, George, *Left Brain, Right Brain*, San Francisco: W. H. Freeman and Company, 1981.

— 4 —

I Can't Help It, I'm Not Responsible

There is a story from the ancient Orient concerning the man who grew tired of seeing his shadow and his footprints following him about every day, so he decided to get rid of them once and for all. He began to run in order to leave them behind. He ran faster and faster, zigging and zagging in an attempt to outwit them, but of course wherever he went he found his shadow at his heels and a trail of footprints behind him. He became more frantic in his attempts, running night and day without stopping for rest, until at last he died of exhaustion—slumped in his shadow at the end of his footprints.

This story captures the relentless, despairing predicament that adult children feel when they get caught up in what we commonly call compulsive behavior. They repeat patterns of activity that they don't understand and would rather not continue, whether it's eating to excess or clinging to an abusive relationship or acquiring more and more possessions or having sex with anyone who's willing or whatever. These compulsive behaviors are not the same as what psychologists would call true compulsions. *Compulsions* are usually more specific individual actions (like washing one's hands) rather than a complex pattern of behavior such as gambling. The kinds of activities we have come to call compulsive are not things we truly feel compelled (that is, forced against our wills) to do. They are more like impulses we get that we allow ourselves to give in to, even though we may think at first that we shouldn't, or that we'd really prefer not to. Once we give in to the impulse, it becomes easier to give in to it the next time, and soon we feel as caught as the man in the legend. How does this happen, and how can we get out of it?

Compulsive Behavior

Even babies show behaviors which could be called "compulsive." The baby who is just learning to pull up to a standing position, for example, will work very hard for minutes on end to get to her feet—then stand there and wail for someone to rescue her because she doesn't know how to get down or how to move herself along the couch she is grabbing onto for dear life. Her parent sets her back on her bottom or on her tummy, and she immediately begins to haul herself to her feet again. This cycle will go on and on again and again until something distracts the baby or until someone interrupts the process ("OK, time for your bath!"), as any parent knows. The baby insists on practicing the same skill over and over with no regard for the consequences, because a baby has no way to think ahead to what a possible consequence might be. She just relentlessly repeats the same pattern until she has mastered the skill and is ready to become immersed in the next one. This is normal behavior for babies as they work on the skills they need to control their bodies.

This kind of repetitive, compulsive activity shows up as toddlers begin to communicate with words and symbols too. The preschooler gets stuck in one kind of response to his situations and finds it very hard to shift gears: for example, a mother offers a cookie to her two-year-old, who responds with "No!" even as he reaches for it. We stick with what we know and are interested in, especially as we are just learning it. As the saying goes, to a kid with a hammer the whole world is a nail.

As babies grow into childhood, this singleminded devotion to practicing new skills continues, but it changes form somewhat over time. Kids still spend large amounts of time and energy working on things which interest them, but their thought processes are developing so that they can now begin to take possible consequences into account (at least sometimes) before committing themselves to a course of action. Their interest in an activity can also be maintained over a longer period of time even if there are distractions. If they are interrupted in an activity, they can return to it with the same intense concentration after the interruption is over, whereas a baby or toddler can't.

One factor which contributes to this process of intense and exclusive attention to our chosen activity is the arousal which our brains experience when we learn something new or when we experience an event for the first few times. The feeling of excited interest we have in a new hobby or skill or pastime sharpens our senses and focuses our attention, increasing activity within our brains. The pleasant sensation caused by this arousal is added to the pleasurable qualities of the event itself to increase our enjoyment, and we are drawn to repeat the action or experience in order to repeat the pleasure.

This may help explain why we are so persistent in practicing a new skill, copying a new fad and so on; and also why our interest in these things can drop off so suddenly, especially in childhood, when they have become familiar enough that the enjoyment we feel no longer gets an extra boost from the novelty of the experience. Once the newness of a fad wears off, we have to rely on the merits of the activity itself to sustain our participation—the "aha!" excitement isn't there anymore to cover for the lack of real value in the activity on its own. (This process of how novelty adds excitement that can't be recaptured once the newness has worn off might also shed some light on the reason that chemically dependent persons are so determined in their pursuit of recreating their first "highs"—and why they are ultimately doomed to fail in the attempt.)

Sometimes, however, we stick with a favorite activity precisely because it's familiar. If there's so much novelty in our surroundings that we become frightened or intimidated by it, familiar things can give us a sense of stability and safety. We don't feel the exciting high of the newness experience, but that's okay because we're already feeling overstimulated by trying to take in all the strangeness of this new situation. We are looking for the comfort which is provided by something we already know. This type of experience releases endorphins in our brains, pain-reducing chemicals which help us feel calmer and comforted in the face of the anxiety we're sensing in ourselves. Sticking with an old favorite helps us feel more prepared for whatever might lie ahead of us.

This natural desire to stick with the familiar for comfort can be strengthened by the magical thinking we all use in childhood, and which we keep the capacity for even in adulthood. Superstitions can result from this process. (A coach wears the same shirt that he was wearing when his team started their winning streak to every game thereafter, for example.) Now we are not only looking for the comfort of the familiar, we're hoping that the familiar behavior will somehow give us added control over the new and unknown factors in a situation. In other words, maybe it will bring us luck. If we get through the new situation successfully, we get back the enjoyment of the "aha!" feeling from this new experience (the boost of novelty) which also strengthens our belief in the truth and value of the superstition. Our logical minds know that the superstition isn't true, but the gut feelings are hard to ignore even so.

In fact, we have so much faith that the familiar tried-and-true methods that have worked before will somehow work again that we stick with them even as it becomes more and more clear that they aren't helping in this new situation. We become more determined: maybe if I try it again, or a little harder, or a little longer this time. If it worked once, it's got to work again. And if it doesn't work, it's because I somehow messed it up, not because there's anything wrong with the old standby. Like the man who tried to outrun his footprints, we exhaust ourselves trying to solve a problem with more of the same cure that didn't work. We forget that if he had stopped running and sat in the shade, he would have made no footprints and no shadow.

Kids at times can display a number of kinds of compulsive behaviors, although any given kind usually doesn't last very long, because so much of the world and of human experience is new to them. They are on a voyage of constant discovery, most of which is pretty exciting and interesting but some of which can also be scary. Three-year-olds will ask for the same bedtime story every night for months. Fifth graders will spend hours watching, playing, reading about and memorizing statistics on baseball or football. Teenagers have to be wearing the latest fashion in the same style and color as everybody else. Kids seesaw back and forth between the exciting compulsivity of the new and the comforting compulsivity of the familiar.

Even as adults, we know that we don't want to get cornered by a recent convert to the joys of running (or nonsmoking or vegetarianism or whatever) because they will, in their new enthusiasm, talk our ears off without noticing our desperate efforts to change the topic. A certain amount of compulsive behavior, on occasion and for limited amounts of time, is normal for all of us. Compulsivity becomes a problem when it does not run its natural time-limited course but instead is prolonged beyond the period when our interest level is intensified by the initial surge of interest and arousal. This may happen for some adult children because they are trying to make up for not having gotten another significant dimension of pleasure from their experiences as they have grown up.

Autonomy

The pleasure we get from new skills does not come only from brain activity or from the natural virtues of the experience itself, such as beauty or grace. Another reason we find new activities and skills enjoyable is because we get to experience ourselves as capable human beings who can do things on our own. We take great pleasure in being able to affect our circumstances instead of having to wait for our environment to react to us. This process begins in infancy, when we really do start out helpless, but it continues throughout our lives.

Everyone who has been around small children for any length of time knows about the "terrible twos." Children between the ages of about 18 months to around three years old can seem to suddenly turn into wailing, strongwilled monsters who defy even the most subtle, well-meant attempts to help them accomplish their chosen tasks. "*I do it!*" is their rallying cry, 24 hours a day. They become furious and are not shy about letting others know it if they have even the slightest suspicion that a grown-up is about to make a choice or complete an activity which they had reserved for themselves—whether they really have the skills to be able to handle it themselves or not. They insist on choosing what to wear according to what strikes them at the moment; never mind that the weather is 20 degrees too hot or too cold for the outfit they selected. They fuss about getting into the car to go visit Grandma, then fuss about having to leave her house when it's time to go home. They eagerly drag a chair over to the counter so that they can peel the carrots, see what's cooking on the stove, wash the dishes. They are intensely insulted when adults don't support their plans. They are reluctant to go to bed at night no matter how tired they are, and greet each day raring to go forth to meet its challenges.

Children of this age are in the first intense experience of autonomy: the ability to act for oneself. Kids who have reached the "terrible twos" have mastered their bodies well enough that they can do a few things on their own, such as walking without having to hold on to someone for balance. This is a heady experience for someone who is not that long past absolute helplessness, and toddlers get lost in the sense of their own power: "*I* do it—I don't have to wait for anybody else." After the frustration of having to depend on others for even the simplest activities, the sense of relief and power must be almost intoxicating.

And yet, despite how exhilarating this new feeling of power is, we still need the reassurance and approval of the people who are the most important to us. For the toddler, that means Mommy and/or Daddy. Kids are constantly urging their parents to "Watch me! Look at this! Are you watching me?" They want to do it themselves—but in front of an audience. They know that they want our attention and approval, and possibly in the back of their minds they also want the security of having a grown-up there in case something goes wrong and they need help. As they grow and become more skilled in handling themselves in a variety of situations, their confidence and self-esteem grows to the point where they feel more secure about doing things on their own, with less immediate feedback from adults.

The experience of autonomy is important in helping to develop a sense of self-esteem. A sense of self as worthy and confident is hard to hatch on its own. It is rather a byproduct of seeing ourselves successfully complete the various things we try to do. It is made up of countless numbers of little and big tasks that we manage to get done, from grabbing the rattle and bringing it into our mouths to getting an A on a spelling test to marrying the person we love to getting all our bills paid each month.

Self-esteem is a lifelong process that has its ups and downs. Just as our opinions on other things change from moment to moment or in different situations, so our opinion of ourselves can vary over time. Self-esteem is not the kind of thing that either you have or you don't. Our self-images are built up of millions of impressions of ourselves as people who can do things successfully, by ourselves and with others. Autonomy is a key issue in the development of self-esteem, one that comes up early in life and continues throughout the course of it.

Babies have no hesitation about trying new things as they work on getting control of their bodies, because they don't have the power to think about what they're doing. All their attention is focused on just doing it. They don't have a sense of others as separate from themselves or as having the power to act independently of what they themselves are working on, so they don't have a sense of needing to call for anyone's approval. For a baby, all of reality is here and now and all one piece. If they're not focused on it right now, it simply doesn't exist. Self-esteem is not a meaningful question for babies.

Young children have more awareness of the world around them, and have more experience of the limits of their abilities as compared with what others can do. They have developed the beginnings of a sense of self: that is, they know that they are separate from others and from their surroundings. They are beginning to understand that they do not have control over what happens around them, although they struggle very hard to gain some control over themselves and to try to exercise it over other people and things. This is when autonomy first becomes an issue, doing *for myself* instead of just doing. Being successful at doing for myself feels good; not being able to do for myself feels crummy. And so the drive for autonomy begins.

Just because we want to become successful at doing for ourselves, however, doesn't mean that we're willing to give up the intimacy that we have with our families, and so we try to include them and their approval in our new pursuits. This is where many codependent adults have experienced problems. As kids grow and struggle with the sometimes conflicting demands of autonomy and intimacy, they need others, especially the most important people in their lives, to cheer their efforts to do for themselves. They need the reassurance that they can become independent without being abandoned, and that being helpless is not the only basis for having a relationship with someone even though that's the way we all start out. They need to hear "That's great, honey!" from the people they love in order to strengthen and affirm their own sense that it really is great to be able to do things for yourself.

Codependent adults may not have gotten this kind of affirmation and reassurance, at least not on a consistent basis, from the important adults and older children in their lives. They may have gotten the message that the price of autonomy is loss of intimacy; that is, that the only way they can get others to notice them is to be helpless or needy or sick. They may have watched others in their families take care of the helpless, sick-acting alcoholic member, while those who are able to take care of themselves get ignored. They may have been punished or ridiculed for the clumsiness and mistakes which their first efforts at taking care of themselves would naturally include. Kids take many of their cues from others, so it's hard for them to feel good about their efforts when no one else seems to.

Balancing Autonomy with Intimacy

Intimacy and autonomy are both important parts of human personality, so we struggle to strike a balance between the needs of each. Codependent people are under the disadvantage of possibly having had to choose which one they would be allowed to develop at the expense of the other. Of course, no one can be perfectly intimate with others or completely autonomous in their actions because we live in the real world with all its limitations. We do have to learn how to adapt and accommodate to various circumstances and needs in our environment, in our relationships, in ourselves. But both intimacy and autonomy need to be developed in order for us to be able to live with others happily and successfully. No one can afford to sacrifice the development of either one for the sake of trying to master the other.

People who try to suppress their natural urge to act for themselves in order to maintain closeness with the important people in their lives live in constant frustration. They see others who seem no more talented or intelligent than they are, yet who have accomplished so much more in school, in sports, in popularity, on the job—and even (in what seems most unfair of all) in relationships. They want to stretch their own wings and try some things too. They feel intensely angry with the ones who hold them back and try to force them to maintain a relationship that is based on dependency rather than growth.

Yet there is fear too, fear that maybe the other person is right and that they probably couldn't really handle themselves if they tried. The other person (my mom, my dad, my wife, my boss, my boyfriend, etc.) knows how to take care of things already; why should I put myself out when I'd probably just screw things up anyway? The longer they stay dependent and helpless, the more they believe that's how they really are meant to stay. Their half-hearted efforts to try something on their own are quickly abandoned, especially if anyone expresses disapproval or questions their abilities to complete the task. Eventually they just give up trying.

Helplessness is very depressing, however, since it runs exactly opposite to our natural tendencies for growth and development. The person who gives up on autonomy in order to maintain closeness with someone who insists on keeping them dependent pays a high price in lowered self-esteem, lack of confidence, and increased anxiety and frustration. Meanwhile, the other person in the relationship gets tired of having all the responsibility for taking care of things, and begins to change the stakes of the game. They feel angry and frustrated too, and begin to send double messages that demand some limited kinds of autonomy ("Can't you even do one simple thing, for gosh sake?") while at the same time maintaining the basic message that helplessness is okay, inescapable, and even desirable in this relationship. ("It's a good thing you have me to take care of you.")

Issue: self-esteem
Level: earliest
Focus: autonomy
Codependent behaviors: • acting helpless in order to have relationships (refusing to be competent) • not letting anyone help me (refusing to be intimate)

If, on the other hand, we try to sacrifice intimacy for the sake of autonomy we can run into serious danger as well. The drive for autonomy begins very early in life, long before our survival skills and thought processes are up to the task of giving us a realistic sense of what we really can handle and what we can't. We need someone who cares about us around, to keep tabs on what we're trying to accomplish and to give us a hand if we need it.

Furthermore, if we choose autonomy at the expense of intimacy, we doom ourselves to a lonely life. The image of the self-made tycoon is very powerful in our society, but the newspapers are full of the stories of successful people whose personal lives are disasters, so much so that sometimes they end up mentally off-balance or even suicidal. We need others not only for physical survival but for our emotional growth and happiness. Communication is so basic to us that some philosophers use our ability to make and use symbolic language as part of the definition of what it means to be human (as opposed to being some other kind of animal). In order to communicate, there has to be somebody else to communicate with, and that means, at some point, dealing with relationships and intimacy. It's not something we can just walk away from, it's a lifelong issue. Intimacy may be the central issue of human life, so any effort to abandon the question in favor of becoming more autonomous is not likely to work very well or for very long. Maybe I really can do it all myself—but it might be more fun if I let you help me, at least sometimes.

Initiative

An issue which is related to autonomy and which develops a little later, as we get some success at doing for ourselves, is initiative: setting myself a task instead of waiting for someone else to direct me. If autonomy is expressed by "*I* do it!," then initiative is expressed by "I *do* it!" As we get more confidence in our ability to act for ourselves, we feel ready to take on the task of setting our own agendas for what we want to do without checking with others for directions or approval. We move from "Watch me, watch me!" to "Look what I just did."

The question of initiative takes autonomy one step further. A small child in the first stages of autonomy sees his mother getting his clothing out for the day and takes over the activity: "I wanna pick!" He didn't start the operation, he is merely trying to take charge of his role in it. An older child who is ready to take initiative will select his clothing himself before his mother even raises the issue. He is making his own choices about what to do, not just making changes in someone else's plan of action. He still may have to go back later and switch all or part of what he has chosen, especially if he took his brother's favorite shirt without asking, but he has started the project by himself.

As kids begin to initiate projects on their own, they get a more solid sense of themselves as competent human beings. Now they are not only choosing roles for themselves, they are taking charge of deciding when and where and how this activity will happen—or at least taking the first steps in that direction. They still need guidance from adults or other kids with more experience, but they are leaving the helplessness of infancy behind them with each successfully completed task.

It is the completion of the tasks which kids initiate that forms the last major piece of this cycle of development. Some authors call this industry, and it basically refers to working on a project all the way through to the end. It's important that kids learn not only to start tasks on their own, but also to work steadily until they are finished. This is a skill that many adult children have not yet developed even though they may have learned how to set agendas for themselves. Adult children may sometimes feel as if their lives are littered with half-done abandoned projects that didn't survive the loss of the "Aha!" enthusiasm. Learning to slog through until we're finished—or to make sure that the project gets completed some other way—is the fulfillment of initiative and ultimately of autonomy.

We might need help to get the job done, though, and under those circumstances it is tempting to turn over the responsibility of completing the task to whoever steps in to help us. That might relieve the anxiety of being in charge all by myself, but it doesn't help us grow into the more adult role of being self-sufficient and responsible. We need to learn how to be accountable for our tasks, from start to finish.

Getting help on a task that a child has initiated on her own will not necessarily make her feel like a failure if the help is given in the spirit of cooperation and learning. Unfortunately, this is not always the way such help is offered. "What the hell are you doing? I never said you could do that! You're screwing it all up—here, I'll do it." Responses like this are all too common to kids' efforts at taking initiative on tasks, for a couple of reasons. One, first efforts are likely to be clumsy and perhaps focused on tasks for which the child really does not yet have all the skills. Two, the adult may be working on his or her own questions of autonomy, initiative, or intimacy at a fairly early level and thus may feel a strong need to be the only one who can do things right. Adults in dysfunctional families are often still thinking, feeling and acting like kids themselves, so they may not be ready to take on a truly adult role such as nurturing the development of the children in their care. So the kids' development starts to lag, and the cycle eventually repeats itself as they too become adult children instead of fully developed adults.

Codependent adults can often recall painful episodes of having been belittled by the important adults in their childhoods for their efforts at becoming autonomous and taking initiative. They remember being ridiculed for being clumsy or doing an incomplete job, yet not getting the necessary instruction on how to do whatever it was correctly. They learn that in order to develop into competent, confident persons it will cost them the closeness they already have (however much or little as that might be) with the adults they care most about. Since intimacy needs are very strong and very basic to human beings, the prospect of not getting them met may be the most terrifying threat we can face. For some of us, that pretty much stacks the deck against ever fully developing our capabilities for self-reliance.

Yet self-reliance is also rather basic to being human, so that a tension may therefore be set up between two equally valid and important types of development. Some of us try to resolve this tension by deciding to remain in the passive, helpless roles we begin with as infants, with occasional timid, brief attempts at asserting ourselves as capable. Others opt for "looking out for #1" and take great pride in being able to do anything and everything for ourselves, even if it means going it alone for large chunks of our lives. Sometimes we ricochet between these two extremes either by parceling out various pieces of our lives between the two areas of development (for example, being a cutthroat self-made man professionally but a possessive, demanding lover) or by allotting certain periods of our lives to working on developing first the one, then the other side of ourselves but not ever really reconciling them with each other—a process which may lead to the kind of emotional upheaval we call midlife crises.

In fact, setting up this kind of either-or choice between autonomy and intimacy is false and unfair. The earlier in a child's life that this false choice is presented as the only alternative, the more that child's development in each of these areas may be harmed. Those of us who are forced to make this decision at a very early age will almost certainly choose intimacy over autonomy, because survival needs are so much more important at that point in our lives, and to choose self-expression over dependence can come dangerously close to being a death sentence.

If we are a bit further along in age and developmental skills when this false choice is demanded of us, two things can occur. One, autonomy stands a better chance of getting some attention in our development, since our very survival is not as much at stake if our intimate relationships suffer a bit. Two, we have already developed some skills and strength in other areas, and will likely be able to use these to help us develop ourselves as individuals, not just as one-half of a dependent duo.

One capability that each of us learns as a part of normal development which may be twisted by this process is the telling of less than the full truth, if not outright lying. Children who are in the "magical thinking" stage of development have a great deal of trouble telling the difference between their wishes and what is really true, as we have discussed. The half-truths and untruths which kids of this age are forever getting caught in are not deliberate attempts to mislead or deceive their parents. Rather, they are the result of real confusion in the child's mind between what's really out there or what really took place, and what I really, really think ought to have happened and wish very hard had happened. Add to this confusion the real fear small children have of being punished by those in authority (namely, their parents or primary caretakers) and you get strong, sincere denials of acts which the parent saw the kid do with his own eyes. Both the parent and the kid are being honest in their point of view: the parent knows the physical act that he saw the child do; the child has magically un-done that act in his mind and "knows" that it never happened.

Older children who are struggling to protect their budding autonomy from their fears of losing intimacy begin to accidentally-on-purpose omit the truth when reporting their activities to a parent or other authority who might not approve of them. They sidestep questions, or answer a question with one of their own, or casually change the subject—anything to get off the hook of having to account for themselves and their activities to someone who might lower the boom on them. A certain amount of this kind of behavior is normal for children of school age and early adolescence, and does not automatically signal a major problem in the child's life or development. Adult children may find themselves getting stuck in this kind of deception, however.

Those who have been asked to make a false choice between their important intimate relationships and their own growth and development as competent individuals try to lessen the unfair pressure of this by using the power to lie. They fall into the habit of automatically embroidering the truth in order to give the other person what they want to hear—or at least, what they think the other person wants to hear, or would want to hear if only they had thought about it—so as to ensure a little breathing room in the relationship to allow for their own self-expression. This habit quickly erases the more mature skill of sharing what one really thinks or feels or has done, so that the adult child soon finds herself telling less than the full truth even when there is no real reason not to. The natural drive to preserve the possiblity for both intimacy and autonomy in one's life gets short-circuited into automatic lying (another of Woititz's characteristics of adult children) and eventually may cost adult children the very intimacy they were originally trying to protect.

It's fortunate that kids have other significant adults in their lives besides their parents, such as grandparents, uncles, aunts, teachers, neighbors, friends' parents, scoutmasters, and family friends. (And this list does not take into account various professionals who also may be involved with children, such as social workers, foster parents, doctors, therapists, and so on.) Among this array of adults, the odds are increased that we will have at least one person who will be interested in helping us develop any given area of our personalities which we may not be getting help with from our parents.

No one adult has to be the be-all and end-all of our developmental progress—as if that were possible in the first place since no adult could ever be perfectly developed in all areas of their personalities. Most of us get more than one opportunity to have someone available, however briefly, to encourage our development in areas that the main adults in our lives may not be able to help us with very well. Many of us also work on furthering our development in these areas even after we have reached adulthood, again with the help of others at times. It's never too late to choose to grow within ourselves, even (or especially!) when it's to help our inner self catch up to our chronological age.

Issue: self-esteem
Level: middle
Focus: initiative
Codependent behaviors: • starting but not following through to the end of a task • "undoing" acts by lying • handing over projects to "helpers"

The course of our development in autonomy, initiative and industry raises the related question of accountability or responsibility ("Who's in charge here?"), which can be a very uncomfortable topic for many of us. Woititz notes as one of the characteristics of adult children that they feel and act over-responsible or under-responsible for people and events in their lives, sometimes both at the same time. The question of responsibility also brings up the connected concept of guilt and its role in shaping our behavior. Are these the same thing?

Responsible But Not Guilty

The processes of autonomy—doing for ourselves, eventually all the way from the start of a task to its full completion—mean that we are developing the ability to take responsibility for ourselves and our needs. We move beyond the absolute helplessness of infancy to being able to help with the care of our own needs, then to being able to take over some or all of our own care, eventually to being able to take care of others. Like the other types of development, this is not a smooth, seamless process like an escalator ride. Rather, there are fits and starts along the way as we try to adjust our autonomous wills to fit with other aspects which go into the development of a sense of responsibility.

A major question in this process has to do with *authority:* who do I see as having the power to decide what should be done (or said, or believed, etc.)? In our infant years this does not come up as an issue because we do not yet have the mental ability to see ourselves as separate from the people and things around us. Everything that happens seems to just happen, since we are not able to take in anything but the immediate present time and place. As we start to realize that we are separate beings, a process that starts with the baby's first smiles of recognition for family members, we must also begin to take into account that our wills do not always agree with the wills of others. This is where the need arises to understand who can decide whose will gets satisfied. That is, who has the authority to decide for me?

For very young children, the answer is obvious: "Mommy said so!" Daddies get some of the authority too, but since the most common experience in our society is that the mother is the primary caretaker, that's most often who is seen as the primary authority. Toddlers don't hesitate to test this authority, particularly when what Mommy said does not agree with what Sammy wants, but if Mommy stays firm in what she decides, the toddler will eventually give in. Maybe not gracefully or right away, but the toddler gives in because Mommy has several things which strengthen her authority: she is bigger and stronger and can enforce her decision, she is his main source of security and he depends on her to make decisions, and she is his primary source of intimacy and affection and he is not about to risk that in a serious way. These same things hold true for whoever is the primary caregiver, including daddies, other relatives, or childcare workers.

As kids grow up and get more mobile outside their homes, another level of authority is added. Now the child is able to take part in other activities in other settings, so new adults are added to the list of caregivers/supervisors. A primary authority who emerges at this time is the teacher, an adult who spends several hours a day in the role of directing and teaching, a task formerly handled pretty much at home. Kids expand their mental list of "who's in charge" and accept the teacher (along with other adults such as police, coaches, librarians, bus drivers, store clerks, and so on) as being an authority who can decide on and enforce the rules.

These other adults tend to still be outranked by parents, however. Our tendency to stick with what we know, along with our bonds of love and loyalty for those who have been present to us when we were helpless, weight the balance heavily in favor of our families. But some shifting of ground takes place, especially when the child thinks that she can play off one authority against another and maybe get what she wanted in the first place. Kids can get quite good at this, especially when the authority at home has not been expressed clearly and consistently by the parent(s), or when the conflicting authorities do not maintain good channels of communication with each other to make sure that they are being quoted and understood correctly.

Further development in assigning authority takes place as kids grow into adolescence, and now their friends begin to take a major role in exercising authority over their decisions and beliefs. "But everybody's doing it!" is often presented as the main argument in favor of some disputed activity by teenagers to their parents. Peer pressure gets stronger than it has ever been, and teenagers are more willing to argue with adults than they have been up to this point. Adults may continue to hold much of the power (love, security, shelter, clothing, the car keys) but the opinions of a kid's peers are a real authority in making personal decisions about beliefs and values. This means, however, that the teenager is still taking his cues from an authority based outside himself.

Issue: self-esteem
Level: later
Focus: industry
Codependent behaviors: • avoiding responsibility with half-truths • refusing to recognize any authority but mine or my friends'

As the person continues to develop (keeping in mind that development in all the ways we have described throughout this book is continuing too), she may reach a point at which she begins to examine her beliefs on their own, independent of what others say. She begins to make decisions on her own authority, based on her understanding and agreement with various rules, norms, and viewpoints which she has learned throughout her life as well as on her own experience. Some of the values she decides to use as a basis for making decisions have come from outside herself, but she is taking the authority to choose to use them.

She has taken these values inside herself and is assuming authority on her own behalf rather than looking to some outside source to direct her. She begins to feel okay about saying "That looks dumb" instead of automatically buying the newest fad, even if her friends are wearing it. She may find herself agreeing with some of her parents' rules and values because of her own conclusions and experiences, although she questions or even forcefully disagrees with other values they hold.

A further step in development on the issue of authority occurs when we spend time comparing and contrasting our own chosen values with the values and standards which other thoughtful persons and groups have developed. We are still reserving for ourselves the authority to set our own directions, but we look outside ourselves to others in order to widen our perspectives in case we may have overlooked some wisdom or circumstance that might be helpful in making our choices. I won't change my mind or my behavior just because you or the group you represent tell me to; but if I am convinced by your group you represent tell me to; but if I am convinced by your logic or your beliefs, I might change some or even all of my viewpoint in order to take your wisdom into account.

The final stage in the development of the concept of authority takes place when I can choose for myself based on ideals that take into account the needs of the greatest number of people, or the greatest good that can be done, or any other universal principle—regardless of whether I will personally benefit from my decision. I feel authorized to choose, but I choose on the basis of beliefs which are much more comprehensive than just my own experience or that of my family, my friends, my church, my nation, or any other single group. I try to bring my own authority into harmony with the widest possible principles of respect, growth, love, and autonomy for all living things and systems. It's not easy, and I am never completely satisfied that I have been able to do this completely in any given situation, but I constantly try to achieve this understanding and to act on this basis.

So, as we grow and develop we see authority first as something outside ourselves but coming ever closer, then as being located within ourselves but with ever expanding resources to draw on for wisdom. Our own desires, however, are located within us from the very first, and this fact can result in tension between acting on getting what we want and settling for what we feel we have permission (from some kind of authority) to do or to have.

It is a natural human tendency to try to do what we want. We choose among our various thoughts and desires for which ones we will act on and in what order, since we can't do everything at once. Even babies have this ability: some newborn in-

Issue: self-esteem
Level: adult
Focus: self-responsibility
Target behaviors: • asserting my authority but consulting yours also • making choices based on universal wisdom

fants will slow or stop sucking in order to pay attention to a new or interesting sound, while other babies in the same room ignore the intrusion. Each infant chooses to do what seems most important to him or her at the time. None of them feel any sense of discomfort about their choices because they are not able to consider any other point of view but their own immediate needs or interests; they have not yet developed the capabilities for that.

As soon as we begin to develop a sense of self, however, we also begin to realize that there are others who are "not me" but who are nevertheless very important in my life and upon whom I depend for almost everything. These others are usually parents, and it is these others who also possess the authority to set rules for me. It is at this point when I may find a tension growing between what I want and what this important other person wants for me, particularly as I begin to develop within the processes of autonomy.

If I act on what I want to do, I get the satisfaction of choosing for myself as well as the joy of pursuing whatever it is that I want. However, in doing this I run the risk of angering my important other. This awakens my fears of losing the intimacy I have with this person and perhaps ultimately being abandoned. (This feeling is called *anxiety*.) It also puts me in direct conflict with my sense that this person does have authority over me and therefore has the right to tell me what my limits should be. Yet I still have a naturally strong inborn urge to follow my own inclinations! If I follow that urge instead of following my sense of who has authority over me, I have to carry the tension from this disagreement around inside me. This distress is what we know as *guilt*.

This tension is very uncomfortable, and we try to do anything we can think of to unload it. The main way to do that is to get either our own wills or the authority figure to back off. Human self-interest being as strong as it is, we usually go to work on the other guy first.

We may get angry with the other person and accuse them of acting not as a pure-minded authority who has our best interests in mind but rather as a cruel dictator. We might try to convince them that what we want to do really is in line with the rules and standards to which they are holding us, and so should be permitted. We might call their motives into question and suggest that they are really only trying to get their own way for their own selfish purposes. We might try to wheedle and coax them into making an exception to the rule "just this once." We might try the silent treatment and see if we can activate their own anxieties about losing intimacy with us. Each of these strategies is designed to do only one thing: to move the tension (between what the authority says should be done and what I want) from my mind to the mind of the other person. That is, if I can make the authority feel that somehow they are not living up to what they think an authority should do, then they will start feeling guilty and leave me alone.

The other possible line of attack is to try to change our point of view about what we wanted to do in the first place. We may try to convince ourselves that it really wasn't all that great or that we didn't feel that strongly about it anyway. We may try to understand and accept the authority's arguments which explain why it was a bad idea. We may accept an alternate suggestion for an activity which will accomplish some or all of what we wanted but which is more acceptable to the authority figure. Or we may just abandon this project and go on to the next one.

The ideal solution, of course, would be to have a calm, rational discussion about what was being proposed and why it has problems in its present form and what would be practical alternatives and when they could be implemented and what else needs to happen to make this project workable and so on and so forth. Unfortunately we live in the real world, and the strength of our feelings and fears about autonomy and intimacy, along with our possible lack of self-awareness about them, usually mean that such a discussion is beyond us without a great deal of preparation and restraint. Add to this the fact that guilt can start to arise at the same time as autonomy and authority issues (beginning at the age of two years or thereabouts), and the probability of resolving guilt with calm discussion seems even more remote.

Adult children know this only too well. Their experience with authority—especially at home, which sets the stage for later expectations of how other authority figures will act—has often been stormy and inconsistent. Not only were the rules usually not clear and not consistent, they have often been enforced by force and threats of emotional and/or physical abandonment rather than by the legitimate use of parental authority. They learn to see authority as arbitrary and controlling and often punishing, instead of as providing the structure and security they need in order to develop. Small wonder that they tend to hold authority figures either in fear or in contempt—or both.

Guilt (the tension between what we want to do and what we feel permitted by some authority to do) can occur no matter where we see that authority coming from. We feel guilty when Mommy confronts us about the crayon marks on the walls. We feel guilty when Coach accuses us of not giving 110% in the big game. We feel guilty when our best friends get mad at us for not backing them up in a fight. We feel guilty when we eat or drink more at the party than we had promised ourselves that we would. We feel guilty when we don't want to test our publicly held beliefs in civil rights by actually letting someone "different" move in next door or teach in our schools. We feel guilty when we try to protect the value of life for all but still see some justification for war or abortion or capital punishment or even eating meat. Guilt is not always a matter of me-vs.-you or us-vs.-them. The tension lies between what we want to do and what we think or feel we should do, regardless of whether the 'should' is coming from outside or inside us.

Building Better Skills

Feeling guilty or anxious is so uncomfortable for us that we try to end the discomfort as soon as we can, using any means that seem promising. If we are aware of what the conflict is that we feel guilty about, we have many options to explore in order to solve the conflict and reduce the tension. Many times, however, we have little or no insight into what we are feeling so bad about, and so our efforts to make ourselves feel better get misdirected. We opt for treating the symptom— the uncomfortable feeling—instead of going for the cure of resolving the guilt. This is where unhealthy compulsive behaviors may start.

An activity which makes us feel better even temporarily is eagerly embraced as the solution for feeling bad, especially when the newness of it gives us added enjoyment. We do the activity again and again in order to hold off the uncomfortable feelings of fear or guilt. As the newness wears off, often the effectiveness of the activity as a distraction does too, so that we find ourselves still feeling bad despite our efforts to feel better. At this point the normal period of initial compulsiveness about enjoyable activities which is natural to humans gives way to the frantic compulsivity which marks our attempts to outrun ourselves, as the man tried to do in the fable. And so we find ourselves "addicted" to shopping, exercise, overeating, sex, chemicals, or relationships rather than dealing with the guilt or anxiety which is driving us.

A more helpful response, because it is more directly related to the root of the problem, is to increase our awareness of ourselves, particularly of our fears and anxieties. We need to know what's bothering us before we can do much of anything about it with lasting effect. There are many routes to gaining greater self-knowledge: joining a self-help or 12-step group, keeping a journal to record our feelings and fears, reading books and articles about how human beings operate, talking things over with friends or relatives, taking a class or a workshop on some aspect of human behavior, going into therapy with a professionally trained helper. The idea is to explore what we think and feel so that we can understand how it relates to what we are trying to do about it. That is, we have to find out what we are trying to fix with our compulsive actions before we will be able to tell why it's not working—and more importantly, to be able to tell what *will* work.

We also can be helped by becoming aware of where we see authority being located in respect to our actions, and to work at locating authority over ourselves within ourselves. If we see others as having responsibility for our actions, we tend to blame them when things go wrong or when we feel bad. We get confused about the boundaries between them and us, just as a small child isn't completely sure where his wishes and opinions end and his parents' begin. We turn over the responsibility for our happiness and well-being to someone else, then often we assume the responsibility for theirs in order to fill the gap within ourselves.

This seems like a fair trade-off at first glance, but the problem is that it doesn't work. Once we mature beyond early childhood, we develop the capabilities to separate from our parents and to function more and more on our own. To attempt to deny that potential in order to hold onto a more childlike dependence is to deny who we are as humans. We begin to learn even as infants that there are boundaries between us and others and that not all others are the same; and we have no choice but to learn to deal with that fact, just as a nine-month-old baby stiffens and fusses when an adult other than Mommy or Daddy comes too close. Trying to ignore the reality of the difference and separation that naturally exists between any two humans does not make it actually disappear. Any attempts we make to pretend that this boundary isn't really there leave us acting under-responsible for ourselves and over-responsible for others. Both are hallmarks of codependent behavior, both are intensely frustrating since they are not accurately reflecting the reality of human dynamics, and both can ultimately be fatal for relationships.

A helpful approach in dealing with the boundaries between people in an appropriate way is to recognize them and to use them to negotiate some sort of compromise between what I want and what the other guy wants. This involves skills at asserting two things: our wants or needs, and our authority to try to meet those wants or needs. *Assertiveness* means standing up for ourselves without knocking anybody else over. It is the middle ground between aggressively insisting on my-way-or-nothing and meekly giving up my position without even trying to get it across, or simply allowing myself to be steamrollered.

Being assertive includes these insights and skills: I must learn to

- know what I want and that I have the right to try to get it;

- know that what you want may be different and that you also have the right to try to get what you want;

- know that I have the authority to act for myself and that you have the same authority for yourself;

- state clearly what I want, what I feel about it, and what I am willing to negotiate on in terms of how to go about getting it;

- ask you for the same information;

- state clearly what I am not willing to give any ground
  on, and respect the limits you set on what is non-
  negotiable for you;

- keep working at the discussion until I get at least part
  of what I want and you get at least part of what you
  want.

The specific ways we work out compromises can change
in each situation. Sometimes we will agree to take turns
("Okay, you watch the game tonight but tomorrow I get to
watch the movie.") or to cooperate on a project ("Help me with
the dishes and then we can both go."). Sometimes we may set
aside our own wishes because of special circumstances or because of the intensity of the other person's feelings about the
situation. ("Well, usually I don't much care for pizza, but I
know it's your favorite, so I don't mind trying that new restau-
rant for your birthday.") Sometimes we may go our separate
ways and agree to meet up again later. ("Sorry, I don't do
opera, even for you. Have a great time and call me when you
get back.") Sometimes the best we can do is to agree to dis-
agree.

But even if we aren't able to work out the perfect solution,
the skills of assertiveness affirm our self-respect, our autonomy,
and our responsibility for choosing and carrying out our actions. They also confirm these issues for our partner in the relationship, and so assertiveness promotes growth for each of
us. These skills can help to strengthen our sense of ourselves
as strong, separate but caring individuals who can act on our
own as capable adults without having to give up close, satisfying relationships.

Few of us really think on a conscious level that we are
being asked to make a choice between being helpless or being
alone, and would be very angry with anyone who put a question like that to us. Yet when we feel torn between intimacy
and competency, deep down we fear that we are asked to make
exactly that choice, and the anxiety which we feel from being
put in this position can enmesh us in compulsive behaviors
that seem to strip us of almost all opportunities for making free
choices. If we work at understanding and working through the
processes of human development, however, we can learn to see
that we don't have to settle for only one or the other. We can

choose to be both responsibly self-reliant and engaged in nurturing, supportive relationships. We can choose to stop running away from our footprints by ourselves, but instead sit in the shade with loved ones until we jointly decide to walk on, footprints or no. That is the choice which gives us the greatest freedom.

"It will be like a man who was about to leave home on a trip; he called his servants and put them in charge of his property. He gave to each one according to his ability: to one he gave five thousand dollars, to the other two thousand dollars, and to the other one thousand dollars. Then he left on his trip.

The servant who had received five thousand dollars went at once and invested his money and earned another five thousand dollars. In the same way the servant who received two thousand dollars earned another two thousand dollars. But the servant who received one thousand dollars went off, dug a hole in the ground, and hid his master's money.

After a long time the master of those servants came back and settled accounts with them. The servant who had received five thousand dollars came in and handed over the other five thousand dollars. 'You gave me five thousand dollars, sir,' he said. 'Look! Here are another five thousand dollars that I have earned.'

'Well done, good and faithful servant!' said his master. 'You have been faithful in managing small amounts, so I will put you in charge of large amounts. Come on in and share my happiness!'

Then the servant who had been given two thousand dollars came in and said, 'You gave me two thousand dollars, sir. Look! Here are another two thousand dollars that I have earned.'

'Well done, good and faithful servant!' said his master. 'You have been faithful in managing small amounts, so I will put you in charge of large amounts. Come on in and share my happiness!'

Then the servant who had received one thousand dollars came in and said, 'Sir, I know you are a hard man; you reap harvests where you did not plant, and gather crops where you did not scatter seed. I was afraid, so I went off and hid your money in the ground. Look! Here is what belongs to you.'

'You bad and lazy servant!' his master said. 'You knew, did you, that I reap harvests where I did not plant, and gather crops where I did not scatter seed? Well, then, you should have deposited my money in the bank, and I would have received it all back with interest when I returned. Now, take the money away from him and give it to the one who has ten thousand dollars. For to every one who has, even more will be given, and he will have more than enough; but the one who has nothing, even the little he has will be taken away

from him. As for this useless servant—throw him outside in the darkness; there he will cry and gnash his teeth.'"

Matthew 25: 14-30

Related Readings

Brazelton, T. Berry, *Toddlers and Parents*, New York: Delacorte Press/Seymour Lawrence, 1974.

Briggs, Dorothy C., *Your Child's Self-Esteem*, New York: Doubleday and Co., Inc., 1970.

Brister, David, and Brister, Phyllis, *The Vicious Circle Phenomenon*, Birmingham, AL: Diadem Publishing, 1987.

Wegscheider-Cruse, Sharon, *Learning to Love Yourself*, Pompano Beach, FL: Health Communications, Inc., 1987.

— 5 —

Oh, Lord, What Do I Do Now?

Some readers who have gotten this far into the ideas in this book may feel just about ready to throw in the towel by now. We develop in so many ways as we grow through childhood and adulthood, in the ways we think and feel and relate to others and express ourselves. It all can look so complicated, it may seem a wonder that any of us ever grow up at all. How could we possibly be expected to keep everything straight and grow up "normal," whatever that might be? It's practically a miracle that we make it as far as becoming adult children, never mind maturing into full adulthood. Is there any hope at all for us?

These worries might be justified, if we had to be solely and completely responsible for both starting up and directing all of our own growth throughout childhood into adulthood. Fortunately, we are not the only directors in this process, and we get help from various sources along the way as we develop.

After all, the natural, automatic impulse of any living thing is toward growing and completing its life cycle. Left on its own without outside interference, for example, a rosebush will produce first leaves, then rosebuds, then full flowers which bloom and drop off, then rosehips which contain seeds which fall to earth and make new plants. We gardeners may choose to interrupt this cycle so that we can get more and better blooms, or so that we can keep the same plant producing flowers for a longer season, but that's not the rose's decision. Assuming it gets enough soil, food, water, and light, it will go on through its cycle automatically, without having to decide whether to make flowers today, or what color to produce, or whether it would be more comfortable in some other part of the garden. Likewise, a puppy will become a dog, an acorn will grow into an oak tree—even mildew will grow and spread over your entire bathroom wall—if it is not prevented somehow from doing so. Nature provides that all living things automatically tend toward growing and maturing through their life cycles, however long it may take.

This means that we have a natural bent toward growing and maturing in all the areas of living that have been discussed so far. This tendency is particularly strong in our earliest years, when we grow so rapidly out of babyhood into childhood. The very earliest levels of development tend to happen whether we pay much attention to their growth or not. No one has to tell a baby to be curious or to search for its mother's face when it hears her voice; these are automatic responses which lead to further change and growth. We are "programmed" for this kind of development when we are born as human beings. We don't have to be in charge of it yet; it just happens, as long as we get basic needs for food, warmth, contact, shelter, and security met.

It is certainly possible to interrupt our normal life cycles even at this early level, however, by not providing for these basic needs. Like any living thing, our survival needs come first before our growth needs, and our energies will be directed first and foremeost toward making sure that we stay alive, if that life is threatened by not having proper care when we are helpless. This is why adults are also "programmed" to find infants so appealing, to help make sure that helpless babies get the necessary care which allows them to concentrate their energies on growing up. The idea of injuring a baby is almost unthinkable to most of us unless our own functioning has been damaged in some way (such as with drugs or alcohol or extreme stress outside the limits of normal daily living). We are outraged if we hear of the abuse of a baby or of a child.

Humans share the instinct to take care of their young so that babies can concentrate their energies on growing and maturing instead of merely surviving. Nature has built this kind of protective reaction into many other types of animals whose young are helpless too. Because of this instinct in our parents, we get a head start on development early in life without having to think about doing it or to take charge of setting directions in how to grow and change. Usually we get to just do it, at least for the first months of our lives.

A bit later on in life, however, when we have grown up enough so that we are no longer completely helpless and dependent on others for our very survival, the situation changes. Now we have begun to develop the skills and capabilities to take over some responsibility for setting the direction of our choices. We begin to be able to have choices for several possible actions in a situation, so that we have to pick out what we will do among more than one alternative. Whether or not we will survive is no longer the biggest question; now the question is how well we will live. The good news is, we get to choose. The bad news is, we have to choose.

It is at this point that development isn't so automatic any more. We have to start making choices about learning the skills that move us along the path of human development. We have to take charge of the process of growing up, although we still need and seek out lots of help and guidance from others around us, especially our parents. We have to take a more active role in shaping our own development. We begin to have to make more important choices.

How do we decide among the possibilities? What basis do we use for choosing one course of action over another, or for choosing which part of ourselves and our growth to focus on in any particular situation? These questions have to do with what we *value* (that is, what we see as important and necessary). They also have to do with what we judge to be right and wrong. Questions such as these reflect our progress in moral development.

Research indicates that we develop through recognizable stages in considering questions of right and wrong, just as we do in other areas of our lives. Some authors have focused on questions of morals and ethics: how do I decide what the right thing is to do in this particular situation? Others have tried to broaden the question to take a look at how these moral values relate to larger concerns about spirituality and the meaning and purpose of life. As in the other areas of developmental theory, however, there is a large amount of agreement and overlap among the various schools of thought which have to do with the development of values and morality. The authors build on each others' work and on developmental theories about thinking and intimacy and autonomy, to try to come up with a model that helps explain how we decide to act on which things in what order—in other words, how we make sense of our lives and our choices. Their work shows stages of development in our ability to wrestle with these questions, just as we grow and develop in other areas as well.

Early Childhood

In our very earliest months, questions of choice do not come up; as we said, growth and development is pretty much on automatic as long as our basic needs are met. By the time we have developed to the point of getting some basic skills in talking and walking, however, we are interacting enough with others that we start to become aware that there are rules that people operate by. We begin to understand that Mommy likes it when I do this or that Mommy gets mad if I do that. We test out this understanding again and again and again just to make sure that we've got it right: "Yep, Mommy spanks me every time I color on the walls."

The way we test for rules is to try a behavior over and over to see what happens. The way we learn the rules is by getting more or less the same response every time we do it. For a young child, this pretty much boils down to "did I get in trouble for doing it or did I get a reward for doing it?" Reward and punishment is the earliest basis on which we decide whether or not to do something.

Remembering how concrete young children are in their thinking, it follows that the rewards and punishments which they respond to will be pretty specific and real as well. A small child will be much more influenced by losing some freedom of movement ("Okay, you have to sit in this chair now if you're going to do that.") or by the gaining or losing of some real object ("Now that you're done fussing, you may have your teddy bear back.") than by more abstract ideas such as "behaving like a little lady." They also find personal attention, especially from a parent or other primary caregiver, to be a major reward for which they will be willing to do a lot.

In fact, personal attention from an important grown-up is so valuable to a small child that they will prefer even unpleasant attention to some other kinds of responses. This becomes even more true when the child does not get enough attention and encouragement for positive behavior. The most treasured reward for a child at the "look at me!" stage of development is to be looked at, hopefully with approval and appreciation. Little kids are also very interested in real objects and experiences as rewards—a cookie, a toy, a ride on the carousel outside the store—and these are powerful motivators as well. Everything else pales in importance next to some one-on-one attention from a loved adult or older child, however.

It follows then that anything which gets in the way of getting that attention is seen as a kind of punishment, which is something unpleasant to be avoided. Banishment to a confined space, whether to a crib or a playpen or one's room or even just the 'time-out chair,' not only keeps me from doing the activity and exploring I crave, it also means that I'm being pretty much ignored, which only adds insult to injury. I will do whatever I need to do in order to get back to my preferred activities, and I quickly learn not to act in whatever way it was that got me in trouble in the first place. Small children learn to respond to other kinds of 'punishments' as well, such as angry looks and tone of voice, having a toy taken away for a certain length of time, and even physical punishments. The most effective punishments, though, are those which involve loss of attention from important others.

Attention from grown-ups is such a powerful reward, in fact, that even unpleasant kinds of attention—getting yelled at, for instance—can be experienced by the child as positive in a way. Sometimes a small child will do something she already knows is against the rules, just to provoke a response from an adult. Getting in trouble is a small price to pay, she figures, in order to escape the bigger punishment of being ignored. Young children are very frightened of being alone and abandoned, and not getting attention from adults feels uncomfortably close to that, unless the child has gotten enough positive attention on a regular basis so that she can develop the trust that she will be taken care of in the ways that she needs to be. Children who have been able to develop this kind of trust have much less of a need to go to extremes of behavior in order to get a response from others.

Using reward and punishment as primary values is about as basic as it gets. If I'm operating at this level, I'm using only myself and my point of view as a basis for deciding what feels rewarding and what is punishment. I'm not considering what the other person thinks or feels about things in order to decide what to do or not to do, although I do accept their authority to act in response to what I do. If I like the way they respond, it's a reward; if I don't, it's a punishment. This can be an effective way to make decisions on how to act, but it's pretty limited too. Most of us are not satisfied to stay at this level of development forever, although we never lose our capacity to be swayed by rewards and punishments no matter how grown-up we get. However, most of us move on to the next level of values and moral decision-making.

This next level comes about when we have begun to be able to take others' separateness into account. As we begin to understand that not everybody thinks and feels exactly the same way at the same time as I do, we also begin to expand our concept of rules for how people's needs are met as having to be fair. In other words, we begin to learn about taking turns and sharing and making sure that other people get something out of the situation too.

This level of moral development is still pretty much self-serving, however. It's the you-help-me-I'll-help-you mentality. Now I'm willing to make sure you get a fair shake even if I don't get my own reward completely or right away, because later you will then have to make sure that I get my fair share too. Not too much later, however—kids at this stage of development are still very concrete in their thinking and can't project too far ahead into the future.

The rewards and punishments that I think about apply to both of us now instead of just to me, but they still have to be pretty specific and real. "I'll be so proud of you if you do that" is not going to be as persuasive a reward as "Help me finish cleaning out the garage first and then I'll take you to the movie you asked to see." It also becomes more important to the child that the grown-up who is doing the rewarding or punishing is someone who they recognize as being in the circle of shared authority: parent, teacher, baby-sitter, relative. Very young children will respond to the authority of almost any adult because they must depend on others for getting so many of their basic needs met. School-age children are less dependent and more self-sufficient (within limits), so they are more choosy about whose authority they will accept. They will take turns or share with others whom they can see as being like themselves and therefore worthy of being treated fairly, and they will accept the authority of those who have been experienced as being part of their normal world. Thus, the regular teacher is an authority; even the substitute teacher gets a certain authority just from teaching in the familiar surroundings of the child's classroom, and especially if the other regular school personnel back her up. A new stepparent, on the other hand, has to go through a period of being accepted as part of the child's world before the child will accept his or her authority to give rewards or punishments, despite what the parents' marriage license may seem to imply.

Defining others as "like me" in order to include them in fair treatment does not have to be as exclusive as it may sound. Kids can be pretty flexible about including others as similar to themselves: because of being classmates, for example, or liking the same baseball team, or being the same height or age, or playing in the same playground, or any one of a thousand other characteristics that might not be enough by itself to convince an adult of the presence of a fundamental similarity. The definitions for "like me" can change from day to day or even hour to hour too, so that my buddy today might be my worst enemy tomorrow and then back to being my buddy by nightfall.

Adult children may recognize some of their current primary value standards among these. While everyone always keeps the issue of reward and punishment as a part of their moral systems, some codependent adults may have gotten stuck here as their main method of deciding how to act. They may be more able as adults to set their own rewards and punishments rather than look to an outside source for them, but they are still operating on the same basic carrot-and-stick method of motivation that young children do. They may feel a need to reward themselves with a hot fudge sundae in order to convince themselves to get the weekend chores done. They may punish themselves with unpaid overtime for having missed a deadline at work. Everything gets totaled up on the balance sheet: do I deserve a punishment or a reward?

Some adult children do in fact still look to others rather than themselves for rewards and punishments and may put others into the role of deciding on the merit of their behavior. They may find themselves pursuing relationships with friends, lovers, co-workers and supervisors who freely offer opinions and advice on what to do or not do, and who are willing to back it up with rewards and punishments (at least in the sense of approval and disapproval). At the same time, these adult children are very concerned about getting their needs and wants met, which means they have to make sure that others notice their behavior so that it can be properly rewarded or punished. So they are constantly checking to make sure that the other people know what their needs are, how important they are, how they can be addressed, etc., etc. It can be exhausting for everyone involved.

Other codependent adults become preoccupied with whether or not people are being treated fairly in interpersonal situations—especially themselves. They're willing to take turns and share attention, but are very aware of how the balance sheets read at any given moment between Accounts Payable (others' needs getting met) and Accounts Receivable (their own needs getting met). Any helpfulness they show toward others is balanced with a hefty dose of "what's in it for me?" They are sincere in their efforts to meet other people's needs and wants, but they rarely do things for someone else without having a price tag attached to it in some way. This is not entirely bad, since it is a system based on fairness, and you always know where you stand with someone who is operating at this level of development. It is, however, still somewhat limited and not flexible enough to account for situations in which the other per-

Issue: deciding on values, right and wrong
Level: earliest
Basis: reward and punishment
Codependent behaviors: • acting "good" only to get approval • making sure others know what I do so I can get proper credit or blame • being "fair" only when I get something out of it

son might not be in a position to return a favor of equal value, now or ever.

Childhood and Adolescence

As children grow a bit more, their daily worlds expand to include other settings and people: school, with teachers, custodians, aides and classmates; clubs, with leaders and fellow members; church, with ministers, musicians, teachers, and other families; recreation programs, with lifeguards, coaches, friends and their family members. These are more formal settings which are now added to the family, friends, daycare, and neighborhood settings with which children are already familiar. The addition of all these new people in their various settings means that relationships and behavior are going to get even more complicated than they have been so far. In order for people to get along together, the rules will have to be spelled out for everybody and we will all have to agree to them. The need for this leads us to the next level of moral development, which is based on two things: personal harmony and explicit laws.

Children at this stage of development are concerned with getting things done, but they can't imagine any way for that to happen unless there is harmony among everybody involved. This means, at the very least, following the rules so that the authority (usually an adult) will not get in your way and may actually even help you. It also may mean living up to that authority's expectations for you and your behavior, in order to win approval and avoid the expression of displeasure which might keep you from getting to do whatever it is you wanted to do.

Kids at this stage are still very person-centered, even though they are developing the capability for logical thought and are beginning to be able to think in abstract terms. Their judgments about how to act are heavily influenced by how others they care about react to them. They are beginning to be able to see themselves from another's perspective—"to see ourselves as others see us," as we mentioned in an earlier chapter—and they know that their view of the other person is not quite the same as that person's view of himself or herself. This gives kids enough distance to see themselves as separate beings but still leaves them very dependent on their relationships with others in order to structure their views on themselves and the world. In other words, I know my view of me is not exactly the same as your view of me, but I wouldn't be able to get a clear picture of myself if I didn't have you around to help me shape it.

For kids, authority has so far mostly been invested in the adults they know personally. They worry about what Daddy will do when he gets home and sees the mess, or what Mommy will say when she finds the broken lamp. Later these concerns get broadened to include what the principal expects of students in our school, or how other church members act and expect us to act as well. Since children are beginning to experience themselves as parts of larger groups, they begin to concern themselves with how the leaders of those groups expect group members to act. They want to meet the group's standards (as expressed by the leader) in order to be included in that group. This, then, marks the rise of group conformity and a real concern with what "they" will say about this or that. Kids become very concerned with meeting others' expectations and keeping peace among group members. (These groups can be defined in concrete terms like "my family" or "my friends," or in more abstract ways like "Americans" or "Presbyterians" or "girls.")

Meeting others' standards can be experienced in a couple of ways. One is by finding out the expectations of the people I interact with within my various groups and working to keep them happy. This is a more personalized approach and focuses on an immediate experience of people as individuals. A second way is by becoming acquainted with the sets of rules which have already been formulated by others who can rightly claim to be a part of this group but whom I may not have met, and using those rules as the standards for my behavior. This is a more abstract, rule-of-law approach. Research indicates that girls may tend to favor the first approach while boys may more often opt for the second, but either or both can be present in any person no matter what their gender.

The fact is, each of these approaches builds from the earlier level of accepting parents or primary caretakers as the real and final authority. The result of each approach is to expand the circle of authority to include others, but the standards which must be met in order for someone new to be accepted as a rulemaker tend to favor those who resemble the image (maybe a little bit idealized) of those whom children first accepted as judges for their behavior. Authorities must still be sincere, trustworthy, knowledgeable, truthful, and so forth, but at this new level of development, not necessarily someone kids know from daily life. This is particularly true as kids use laws or rules as a basis for judging right and wrong; they don't have to be friends with the Commissioner of Baseball in order to agree on what constitutes a force-out.

This stage of moral development includes a wider set of options for seeking answers to the question of right and wrong, but it still lodges final say-so outside the person. It also remains, for the most part, the result of some unconscious assumptions. Kids at this stage tend to take for granted the rightness of those whom they see as their authorities, and don't much question whether a rule is right, or fair to those who might be outside the group. It seems perfectly obvious that they should listen to the coach, or that the teacher is correct about how things happen in nature, or that the minister knows what God would want. They don't spend much time defending these standards because any fool could see that they're right—and if you can't see it, you must be cuckoo.

On the other hand, kids at this stage experience their lives as happening in circles which are somewhat separate from each other, although there's a certain amount of overlap between them. My school friends might also be in Brownies with me, for example, but the Brownie troop probably also includes kids from the other class, and the troop leader is not my teacher. This means that there are several different sources of authority (and therefore of rule systems) for kids in their daily lives, which may be mostly similar but probably have some important differences among them as well.

Experiencing life as a series of kind-of-overlapping-but-really-pretty-distinct circles grows out of the earlier experience of seeing life as a series of separate episodes rather than as the continuous flow we later think of it as being. This is how kids experience life before they develop a sense of the continuous movement of time. There are a couple of important results of this sense of things as being basically disconnected. One, it strengthens the knowledge that how others see us and how we see ourselves are not the same, because since nobody is in all of the areas of my life with me, so nobody has the complete picture of who I really am the way I do. Two, the various rule systems we adopt in the different areas of our lives are not looked at too closely, because then we would have to confront the differences or even the contradictions among them, and kids don't have the skills they need in order to be able to do that just yet. So, we accept our authorities as obviously correct and don't try to explain things in too much detail, and if we get to some contradiction which doesn't make sense, we shrug and say, "I guess it's just a mystery."

It is very common for adults, especially but not only adult children, to reach this level of moral development and not go beyond it. This is a very practical way of addressing questions of right and wrong and of what's important, and it works well in many if not most situations of daily life. The value of many of the rules of everyday life are in fact pretty obvious, from putting things away when you're finished with them to covering your mouth when you sneeze to not interrupting the person who's speaking without a compelling reason. Depending on how broadly we define the groups whose rules we accept, we might well be able to live comfortable, productive, happy lives simply by following the laws set out for us by governments, religions, social agencies, local customs, and other groups, and/or by meeting the personal expectations of the people who represent their authority.

The pitfalls in limiting ourselves to this stage of development are also clear, however. No rule can cover every possible situation, and so every rule will have exceptions or special circumstances which keep it from answering questions for us in a fully satisfactory way. Likewise, meeting the expectations of others in authority would be much simpler and more straightforward if they were not just regular people like ourselves, with all the personal problems and needs that we have too, which can distort their judgment and cloud their thinking just like us.

Then too, the contradictions and gaps among the various sets of rules and authorities that we live by get harder and harder to ignore as time goes on, yet the tools of this stage of development don't give us much to work with in trying to make sense of them. Relying on outside authorities relieves us of a lot of the responsibility for figuring out how to make decisions on what to do, but we pay a price for this "freedom." Adult

Issue: deciding on values, right and wrong
Level: middle
Basis: laws for personal harmony
Codependent behavior: • pleasing authorities no matter what • ignoring contradictions among the rules • acting very differently based on where I am or who I'm with

children who find themselves feeling jerked around by others or hemmed in by the rules without being able to say why or how, are paying that price.

Late Adolescence and Adulthood

People who are at the level of development we have just been examining define themselves and their standards for behavior by the groups, rules and authorities to which they are loyal. They do not see themselves as having an identity outside their group memberships; that is, they can only understand themselves in terms of being Black, or Buddhist, or Swiss, or a veteran, or a member of some other particular group. Some others of us, however, are able to take a step outside their experience of themselves as a member of various groups, to begin to examine the rules and standards of these groups and decide whether or not to accept them as guides for themselves. Such people have moved on to the next phase of moral development.

At this new point, we develop the perspective of seeing ourselves first and foremost as individuals. We still recognize various groups to which we belong and feel loyal, but we no longer accept their rules and authority without question. Now we have to go through the process of internalizing these standards, of taking a look at them in comparison with our own experiences, opinions, and thought processes to see if they make sense for us and for our particular circumstances. As a result, the loyalties we feel to our various groups become a matter of "This is what I choose to be," whereas at the previous stage they could more accurately have been expressed, "Of course I am (one of this group)—what else would I be?"

Persons who have reached this stage in development are firmly rooted in logical thought processes, and these become very important in evaluating the rules, standards, and expectations of other people and groups. Things have to make sense, to "hang together" logically in order to satisfy the individual now. This is not to say that emotions are not important, because they always are important in human experience, but it does mean that the person is more likely to be aware of processing moral issues on the basis of thought rather than of feeling. At this stage it is not enough that something feels right; we want to be able to express the larger principle behind it.

In the earlier stages, the rightness of the group's standards seemed obvious, not needing any explanation. Now, we reach the level of being able to take a look with a critical eye at the group standards we hold. We recognize that not everyone might accept these standards automatically, and that logical, well-meaning people might question them against other standards for behavior. This means that we must first consider and then explain—to others or just to ourselves—why we accept these standards as right.

We can resolve this obligation to defend our moral standards in either of two ways at this stage. Some choose to separate themselves from their previous unquestioning acceptance of various group standards and substitute a sort of situational ethical code instead that says, in effect, "Everything's relative; how I choose to act depends on the situation." Their rules for right and wrong will vary, sometimes a lot, according to the circumstances or the people involved. A second way to make sense of moral questions at this level is to try to evolve a set of principles which takes into account the contrasts and differences of other individuals and groups who are not part of my own chosen groups. This process takes a certain amount of effort over time, and at this stage people's understanding of moral positions which are different from their own is likely to be somewhat simplistic, limited by the level of their ability to get distance from their already accepted norms. They are sincerely trying to develop ideals based on justice for all, but they are as yet still limited to some extent by the built-in biases of their self-accepted groups.

Codependent persons can get tripped up, if they get locked into this stage, by over-enthusiastic insistence that the systems which make sense to them will therefore work for everybody. They've figured it out, and while they will stop short of demanding that you accept their logic, they can be pretty darn insistent about drawing parallels between your experience and theirs and "proving" that their particular norms are the way to go. They are aware of perspectives which might be different from their own, but in trying to make sense of these they may unintentionally reduce them to simplified, cartoon-like forms that are almost caricatures of the real positions. These people are not mean-spirited bullies; they are making genuine attempts to make sense of life and to find a moral system which works, and they are sincere in wanting to help others in that same task.

On the other hand, some adult children get so individualistic that they refuse to acknowledge almost any universal norms. "I can't tell you how to live; I only know what works for me," is their reply and their defense in any discussion of moral questions. In fact, they'd like to end the discussion as soon as possible rather than have to explain their stand on an issue. They take moral questions seriously and think about them, but they feel incapable of finding moral principles which are broad enough to cover the demands of special groups or situations. For them, every moral act or decision is limited and explained by the specific circumstances which surround it. Thus, every situation must be considered and decided on anew, which can leave these folks feeling frightened and exhausted from having to reinvent their standards all the time.

If we can avoid these extremes, this level of moral development can be a satisfying and highly functional stage at which to remain. Living one's life according to group norms which have been freely chosen after serious individual reflection is not a bad way to go. It provides both for taking responsibility for oneself and for considering how others think, act and feel.

The development of our abilities to make moral decisions up to the point we have discussed so far could be summed up this way: we move from making decisions based on forces outside ourselves which we cannot control (do I get a reward or a punishment?) to making decisions which we can influence a little (be nice to me and I'll be nice to you) to making decisions that fit in with everybody else's (meeting expectations and following the rules) to making decisions based on what I accept as right from a particular framework of standards (this is what works for me). Sincere, conscientious people can be found at every stage of this process of development, trying to live according to what they think or feel to be right and fair and important. The specific situations or behaviors which they are trying to decide about change every day, sometimes unpredictably, no matter at what stage they are operating. What develops in a recognizable order over time is *how* they make their decisions—what processes they use to go about choosing answers, not which answers they choose.

Issue: deciding on values, right and wrong
Level: later
Basis: making individualized choices
Codependent behaviors: • if it works for me, it's right for you • deciding every question separately, without any general norms

That is, two people who are at the same stage of moral development might have very different sets of ethical standards and might choose opposite courses of action when faced with the same situation. For example, one man might enter combat and fight the enemy because the rules of society say that he must do what his country and his commanding officer tell him to do. Another man might refuse to serve in that same combat situation because the rules say "Thou shalt not kill." These men have reached opposite conclusions, but they each used the same kind of process to make their decision: "what does the rule say?"

On the other hand, two people who make identical moral decisions may be doing so for very different reasons, and thus are at different stages of moral development. I might stop at a red light because I'm afraid I'll get a ticket (that is, I'll be punished) if I don't; you might stop at that same red light because that's the law and there would be chaos in the streets if people routinely ignored the traffic laws. We both end up stopping at this light, but you're more likely to stop at lights even when there's no one else around because you're following the rules, whereas I'm more likely to go through them if I think I can get away with it without a punishment. You may have felt the way I do in the past, but now you've moved beyond that stage where I still am—even though someone watching our behavior at this particular light would not see any difference between us.

Moving Ahead

Research has indicated that people who continue to develop their moral reasoning as adults may reach another stage of ability in moral decisionmaking. At this next stage of development, they begin to integrate other voices or outlooks with the one they worked so hard to perfect in the more individualistic stage we have just been discussing. They become more aware of and accepting of the contradictions within themselves as persons, which gives them increased empathy with ideas or standards or people which contradict notions they may have held dear up to now. They move closer and closer to a more universal understanding of the values they cherish rather than being locked into viewpoints which represent mostly their own experience. Researchers say that the achievement of this level of moral development rarely comes before around age 30, more often occurs during middle age, and may not happen at all. It does not require extra education or unusual experience in order to get there. It involves reclaiming and rethinking one's past and the unconscious assumptions from all the various sources in one's past which have shaped the person to where they are now.

People who are at this stage in making moral choices are in touch with the complicated nature of truth as a paradox—that is, that things which appear to contradict each other may nonetheless both be true. Those of us who are at earlier stages of moral development spend a lot of time trying to explain or ignore the paradoxes we run into in our lives, just as the six blind men argued about their apparently contradictory experiences of the elephant. Persons at this later stage accept these contradictions as necessary to the complex nature of reality. In a sense, they are better able to begin to see the whole elephant.

We need to achieve a deep self-awareness and a broad understanding of others in order to progress this far in making value judgments. Our capacity for logical thought must expand to include the ability to consider opposite statements both separately and together, and to accept both without reducing or rejecting either. Our understanding of symbols—such as my country's flag, for example—grows to include both logical and emotional appreciation of not only what they mean to me personally, but what they might mean to someone totally different from me, and how each of our understandings is not only true but necessary for really getting to the true meaning of the symbol. The push for justice grows to include not only an understanding of what must be done in order to secure just and fair treatment for everyone, but also the necessity of actually carrying out whatever actions one can in order to make sure that justice takes place. In this stage, there is no gap between thinking about what seems to be morally right and actually doing it. Those at this stage are willing to "put up or shut up."

People with this outlook will be less limited in their understanding of the groups to which they see themselves belonging and being loyal to. They are apt to define themselves in more global or universal terms, as a member of humanity or of creation or of the forces of life and love. They are not necessarily great leaders or presidents of large corporations; they may not have great power or influence or even be known outside their circle of friends or their hometown. Yet they somehow seem to know that we're all in this game of life together, and they have more than the usual amount of compassion and empathy for others, whether it's readily obvious that they have something in common with those others or not.

While not everybody grows to this stage of moral development, we may be fortunate to have known someone during our lifetime who has achieved this kind of integration: perhaps a grandparent who always seemed to have time to talk and to take the wider view of our troubles, or a teacher who could reach out and find a way to touch even the most walled-off problem kid, or the neighborhood handyman who could help you fix what was wrong inside while he helped you complete the household maintenance. They seem to be able to see beyond themselves in a way we would have no reason to expect, given the ordinary circumstances of their lives. They may not be geniuses or rich or powerful. They may never appear in an article in *Reader's Digest*. Yet they show a wisdom beyond their experience, and they call us to grow beyond our current selves as well.

As idealistic and larger-than-life as this stage sounds, nonetheless there are limits to the wisdom which those who are at this stage can achieve. They appreciate the paradoxes of life, but they are still bothered by them. When push comes to shove, there are groups to which these persons do feel greatest loyalty, and it is to those groups that they will turn if forced to make a choice. There can be yet another stage of moral development beyond this one, a stage that only a very few persons ever achieve, in which one truly becomes a "citizen of the universe" and makes moral choices based on the most universal principles of Being and Love. This is the rarest and highest level of moral development.

Persons of this level seem to give off an aura of incredible inner peace, and yet they may make the rest of us profoundly uncomfortable. They have resolved the paradoxes which those of us at previous levels of development either ignore, struggle with, or appreciate. They don't see the world with themselves at the center, as the rest of us do. Rather, they see the community of life and being as the central reality, and see themselves as just one part of it.

In a sense, they have come full circle to an understanding of moral questions as being concerned with values and realities which are outside themselves, and yet the circle has been turned inside out. At the starting point, we are concerned with getting our own needs met, and rightly so since we cannot meet them for ourselves. Yet at this highest stage of moral development, we realize that our needs are already being met in the largest scheme of things, and that our role is to do our part in the grand design of meeting all needs. Babies experience life as a seamless whole with themselves at the center. These few special people know with certainty that life is a seamless whole with love as the center.

Such persons make moral choices on the basis of loyalty to Being rather than to any specific group, even a group as large as "humanity." Their actions are aimed at trying to make real and actual the essential oneness of all that exists. They are aware, in a very fundamental and present way, of the constant gift that is life and their mission is to help others realize the wonder of this gift in real ways.

It is hard to try to describe this stage without sounding like some kind of loony poet, because so few of us have achieved this level of moral awareness on any kind of consistent basis; even so, we may be able to recognize it in others, and we ourselves may have brief flashes of this kind of insight. It is tempting to dismiss this stage with a shrug and the argument that, "well, we can't all be Mother Theresa." That's part of what makes us so uncomfortable about people who have progressed to this stage of moral reasoning. They show us that it is indeed possible to get to this level of understanding of what is right and important, and if it's possible, then don't we have the obligation somehow to try to get there ourselves? What a frightening thought!

Issue: deciding on values, right and wrong
Level: adult
Basis: choosing to act by universal truths
Target behaviors: • acting on moral standards, not just thinking about them • accepting others as part of the same universal group as me

Building Better Skills

As always, the first step in continuing our development as adults is to get a sense of what the big picture is so that we know in what direction to head. If we can locate ourselves along the path of development, we know what we've already accomplished and what we can expect to encounter next. In terms of moral development, we can begin to see how to use the skills we have already developed or are currently working on in other areas of life to assist us in expanding our awareness of ourselves and others, as we grapple with the questions of what is right and true and important.

As we have seen, the groups we see ourselves as being part of and loyal to play a big role in our moral development throughout life. It is helpful, therefore, to spend some time thinking about these groups and trying to make conscious choices about them.

- Why do I feel like a part of this group?

- Why do I stay?

- What do I gain from this group? What do I give to it?

- Do the rules and assumptions of this group make sense—for me? For others?

- How do they compare with the rules of other groups to which I belong?

- Are the leaders or spokespersons for this group faithful to the real values of this group? Can I trust them?

- Are there other groups who hold the same values that I/we hold, that I could be part of too?

Keep in mind that values do not come only from our membership in the kinds of groups that we already think of as being concerned with moral questions. While it is true that our values are shaped by family and church and school, they are also affected by clubs, friends, leisure groups, gangs, office co-workers, the people who drive the freeway during rush hour with me (is it acceptable to cut someone off in heavy traffic?), television and radio programs—well, you get the idea. The more awareness we develop about the many groups to which we belong and the standards which each one represents, the better position we will be in to make conscious choices about evaluating these standards, and evaluating ourselves and our behavior in relation to them.

There is an idea called the *shadow* in the psychology which was developed by Carl Jung, and it refers to the abilities which are possible for us to develop but which are not our natural strengths or talents. In other words, our shadow side starts out as a weak or undeveloped area of our personalities and skills which we don't even see as a real part of ourselves, and we have to put attention and effort into bringing it even into our awareness, much less into its full potential. This is in contrast to the process of developing our natural strengths and talents, which tends to be more automatic since we use these often and easily. The paradox of the shadow side, Jung says, is that we are likely to find our greatest success and creativity when we use this lesser-developed, less "natural" area of skill and perception to address an issue we are struggling with.

Jung's concept of the shadow may be particularly useful as we consider how to move ahead in moral development. As we have seen, moral development refers not to the content of our values and ethical decisions but to the process of choosing them. That is, it has everything to do with how we choose and not as much with the specifics of what we choose. When we are faced with choosing how to act or what to emphasize in our lives at any given time, it may be helpful to step back from the tried-and-true, the ingrained habit, the automatic assumption about the ways we've thought or acted or felt up to now. Since values are about choosing, this may be the arena where taking the road less traveled among our usual skills and perceptions may be of the greatest help.

Although we may continue to choose the selfsame behavior in the end, as we expand our methods and bases for making choices about our actions we make progress in moral awareness and open up a greater variety of options for our choices. We know that in the physical world, anything of substance throws a shadow when exposed to a source of light. We might think of ourselves as using that shadow to broaden the influence of the substance of our moral decisions. Developing and using the fullness of the power to make the most creative choices to serve the greatest good for the largest number of people seems a worthy goal for any adult.

Three umpires were asked about the art of making calls at home plate during a baseball game.

"Well," said the first, "some are balls and some are strikes, and I call them the way they are."

The second answered, "Well, some are balls and some are strikes, and I call 'em the way I see 'em."

The third umpire gave the questioner a long, level gaze. "Some are balls and some are strikes," he said, "but they ain't anything until I call them."

Related Readings

Bowden, Julie and Gravitz, Herbert, *Genesis: Spirituality in Recovery*, Pompano Beach, FL: Health Communications, Inc., 1988.

Covey, Stephen R., *The 7 Habits of Highly Effective People*, New York: Fireside/Simon & Schuster, Inc., 1989.

Kroeger, Otto, and Thuesen, Janet, *Type Talk*, New York: Delacorte Press, 1988.

Wholey, Dennis, *Becoming Your Own Parent*, New York: Doubleday, 1988.

— 6 —

So, How Do You Feel?

Marilyn vos Savant is listed in the *Guiness Book of World Records* as having the highest documented IQ of any living human being. To most of us, then, that means she is the smartest person in the world, and on that basis she has a syndicated column in the Sunday newspaper supplement. One of her readers wrote in to ask, "In your opinion, what's the best thing and the worst thing about computers?" Marilyn answered, "1) They have no feelings, and 2) they have no feelings."

Many of us share this conflicting feeling about the value of our emotions. They can be uncomfortable and can really complicate situations in which we'd like to be our calm, level-headed best. On the other hand, nothing frightens us as much as the coldly logical, unfeeling foe who operates with robotlike precision in movies and television. *Star Trek's* otherworldly characters Mr. Spock and, in the next generation, Commander Data are accepted as part of the "good guys" not because of their impressive logic and brainpower but because their thought processes are tempered with emotion in spite of themselves. Arnold Schwarzenegger's character in *The Terminator* had to be changed in the sequel into having some possibility for emotion, in order for us to be able to root for him as he battled the new bad guy: a robot who is even more unfeeling than Schwarzenegger had been in the first movie.

We instinctively know that emotions and their expression are at the heart of human experience. What's the first question a reporter asks as he shoves the microphone into the face of the just-released hostage, or the triumphant champion, or the bereaved spouse, or the survivor of a disaster: "How do you feel about all this?" We ignore emotions when it's convenient for us to do so, but feel enraged when someone else ignores or

113

hurts our feelings. We write songs about them and endlessly try to sort out and understand them. Newborn babies show evidence of possessing emotions, and even animals act in ways that seem to show feelings like sadness or jealousy. Just where do feelings come from, anyway? Do we develop in stages of capabilities for feelings the way we do for thought processes or moral decision making?

The Biology of Emotions

We usually talk about feelings as coming straight from the heart, but most of us already know that this is just a figure of speech. In reality, our feelings are a function of activity within our brains. Several structures within our brains are involved with the experience of emotions, especially the *amygdala* (a very small, almond-shaped structure that seems to be our "emotion headquarters") and the *thalamus* (a larger structure which processes sensory information). The *hippocampus* (another structure which sort of nestles around the other two), which is important for gaining and storing knowledge, also plays a role in our emotions, although less of one than we had originally thought before the most recent research findings. All of these structures, which together make up what is called the *limbic system*, are buried deep within our brains, in the part which some call the "old brain." Also included in the "old brain" is the *brain stem* (basically the very top of the spinal cord, the big nerve which runs down through and is protected by our backbone), which is sometimes called the "reptilian brain." These less-than-flattering names refer to the fact that this part of our brains evolved very early among living creatures, and that many kinds of animals of complex enough development have brains which demonstrate the same abilities that this part of our brains has.

The "old brain" is in charge of the functions which allow us to survive: heartbeat, breathing, digestion, sleeping, reproduction, gathering and sorting out sense information. It directs and coordinates physical activity on the most basic level. The responses which are supervised by this part of our brains are more or less automatic or instinctive. We don't have to think about them in order for them to happen—they're part of the preprogrammed material we are born with. Damage to this part of the brain means that we cannot survive unless some outside technology takes over these automatic functions for us. It's not surprising, therefore, that the old brain is buried deep within our skulls, surrounded by bone and other tissue for maximum protection.

By far the largest part of the human brain is the *cortex*, the wrinkly, gray, two-sided organ that most of us picture when we hear the word *brain*. The cortex, which surrounds the limbic system and covers the brain stem, is the most recently evolved part of the human brain. It takes care of conscious processes like logical thought, self-awareness, decisionmaking, planning, creativity and dreams. What we might call our higher functions, our sense of self or identity, are governed by the activity of the cortex. Humans have the most highly developed cortex of any living being on earth.

Since the brain stem, the limbic system, and the cortex are all part of the same brain, all of these parts can communicate with each other. Even though we aren't aware of our heart's beating—an activity controlled by the brain stem—most of the time, for example, we are able to bring it into our awareness— an activity of the cortex—and even to perform conscious acts like meditation or slow deep breathing—also directed by the cortex—in order to slow it down. We don't usually experience ourselves as sectioned off into separately-controlled parts; our brain works most of the time as a unified system operating in quietly busy harmony.

Our knowledge about brain anatomy and function has increased so rapidly, especially in the second half of this century, that it seems to be almost an explosion. Much of the research has focused on the cortex and on its functions of thinking, memory, and perception. What we have learned about the differences between the functions of the two halves of the cortex (right brain/left brain differences) came from this research. More recent work is focusing on emotions and their relationship to thought processes and physical processes, and how this relationship shows up in various kinds of brain activity.

As we said, the "headquarters" for emotions seems to be the amygdala, which is part of the limbic system. Like the rest of the "old brain" it is already functional even at birth. One of the things it does is to work with the rest of the brain to help direct movement of the muscles which change our facial expressions. Studies indicate that the faces we make to express basic emotions like fear, happiness, disgust, sadness, and anger seem to be the same throughout the world despite cultural differences we may have in expressing these emotions by words or gestures, and that even very young babies can recognize and respond to these universal facial expressions. Other studies indicate that the automatic, brain stem-controlled responses which are characteristic of the various emotions—the cold sweat and churning stomach of fear, for example—can be called forth not only by the experience of that emotional state, but also by the mere memory of a vivid experience of that emotion, or even by just arranging one's face muscles into the appropriate expression even if one has not been told what emotion they are showing.

Our "old brains" don't develop very much after birth, so the presence of our emotions and the automatic physical responses to them do not change very much thereafter either. Our cortexes, on the other hand, develop a great deal for many years after birth, and this physical development plays a role in what we call emotional development as well. Since the three parts of our brains operate in harmony and constantly communicate with each other, the thinking processes directed by the cortex have an influence on and are influenced by the feeling processes directed by the limbic system and the brain stem. This means that while the facial expressions of our feelings may not change much over time or place, the additional ways in which we choose to express our feelings—the gestures, other actions and the words—may very well change. Furthermore, our understanding of various circumstances and situations, which calls forth our emotional response, will almost certainly develop over time as our thought processes develop, and this will affect our emotional expression too.

The process of emotional development, then, is not so much a matter of developing the capacity to feel or to be able to express feelings; we already have that ability. Rather, it is a matter of learning to temper the expression of the pure feelings which we experience from babyhood onward with our developing awareness of others' points of view, of additional factors to take into account, of possible dangers resulting from sudden, violent outbursts, and so on. We will grow in learning the different shades and tones of fear, anger, happiness, disgust, and sadness, but the basics are already in place. The kinds of development which we have been looking at in previous chapters play major roles in our developing appropriate forms of emotional expression.

We can see the effect that limited development of thinking processes has on emotional expression by watching how small children express their emotions. Little kids don't have very big vocabularies, but they sure know how to get their point across when they're angry or sad, for example. Their body language is unmistakable; not just the facial expressions we talked about before, but their entire bodies get into the act of letting the emotion out. Shoulders droop, lips tremble, eyes fill with tears before the first sob ever escapes a sad little child. Eyes flash, the arm is drawn back and cocked as a warning, eyebrows bump into each other, muscles tense, the head is lowered forward and jutted toward the object of a small child's anger— any words are just icing on the cake as far as getting the message through is concerned.

Small children instinctively use their bodies to send messages of strong emotion because they have few other tools to do so. Their abilities to reason and to share their thoughts are very limited, as we have seen, but their emotions have been present since birth. Kids throw tantrums to express themselves because they don't have many other options, and one of their parents' first tasks is to help them learn how to express themselves in ways which are more clear and constructive toward actually solving the problem.

This process takes a while, but kids are usually open to learning it, because their tantrums scare themselves as well as the rest of us. Children don't like the sensation of being out of control, and they rely on their parents and other authorities to help them maintain safe boundaries. When children do lose control of themselves and hit or throw things or get into a hair-pulling match, the damage done is not often serious. Kids are not strong enough under normal circumstances to hurt themselves or others seriously (assuming that they are receiving enough supervision so that they cannot get at or into things which pose a sudden, real danger, like matches, for instance). We have time to teach them ways to express themselves which use higher-level skills than screaming before they will have the physical strength or quickness to pose much of a threat to themselves or others. Teach them we must, however, because learning how to express ourselves with language is not an automatic process, and the consequences of a twenty- or thirty-year-old throwing a tantrum, when he or she can have legal access to things like guns and knives, are far more serious—possibly, deadly serious. Adult children often struggle with the painful and problematic results of never having been taught how to put their emotions into words instead of expressing them physically; or, if the thought of losing control of themselves in a tantrum is too frightening or costly, not expressing their feelings at all.

So, as kids grow and acquire the skills of language, they need to learn how to put feelings as well as ideas into words. Children can be taught the names of emotions, and they easily learn to use these in everyday conversation from early childhood on. The words they use and the way they tell about what happened to trigger the feelings they're sharing will reflect the stage of development at which their thinking processes are operating. But even the earliest levels of mental development allow for clear, specific expression of what we're feeling. Being young and riled up may make it harder to come out with a calm, abstractly reasoned report, but they are no excuse for refusing to admit that we have feelings, or for acting them out instead of talking them out.

Emotions and Survival

Our first and foremost objective as living beings is to survive, and human development is geared toward making as sure as possible that the odds are in favor of that. One of the instincts we are born with in order to further that cause is our strong drive to avoid pain and to seek out pleasure. Pain is seen as a warning of danger, a message of a threat to our survival. We are programmed to react instantly to pain and to take immediate action to remove it by whatever means available. Our thought processes, our emotions, and our behaviors all work together to reduce or eliminate pain and to replace it with pleasure, if possible.

It was the study of the response to pain in humans and in animals which led to the discovery of endorphins, those brain chemicals which numb pain. Research has shown that one of the ways endorphins ease our pain is by dulling our attention to the pain itself so that we can redirect our focus toward removing the source of the pain. That's why people who have been hurt in life-threatening situations are often unaware that they have been hurt, or how seriously, until after they have been able to remove themselves from the fire or the rock slide or the assassin, when their endorphin levels drop and the pain which they suddenly feel lets them know that they have an injury to take care of. It is more helpful for their survival that they ignore any painful wound until they have dealt with the immediate problem and are out of danger. Once that has been accomplished, however, it becomes necessary for survival that they attend to their injuries, so the endorphins stop and allow the pain to signal the need for care and recovery.

Other research has found that stress, or psychological pain, can trigger the release of endorphins in our brains just as physical pain can. The more trapped we feel by the stressor, the greater the rise in the level of endorphins. The role they play seems to be to block our awareness of the inner pain, which otherwise would claim all of our attention, so that we can use our mental energy to concentrate on finding a way out of the painful situation. For our early cave-dwelling ancestors, stressors were most likely to be physical dangers: the clan from over the hill coming to attack, or the cave bear about to dispute the ownership of the cave, or the need to chase down dinner in the hunt. In our society, stress tends to come more from mental sources or psychological forces, such as unpaid bills or unkept promises. Either way, the reaction of our brains seems to be to handle the stress in the same fashion. First, our awareness is drawn to the pain and its source so that we realize that we have a problem, then the endorphins kick in to dampen our awareness of the pain itself so that we can assess the whole situation and escape the danger.

When our attention is first drawn to a problem, our brains are aroused to pay closer attention. We often experience some form of fear at this moment. If the threat is specific, such as a physical threat, our bodies go into overdrive and prepare for the classic "fight-or-flight" response of flooding our bodies with hormones which speed up heartbeat and breathing, increase blood pressure, send energy to our muscles, and prepare for the release of endorphins, to get us out of harm's way. Psychological stress is often much less specific, however, and the fight-or-flight surge of hormones does not help us to deal with the complexity of figuring out what a newborn baby is howling about, for example. When the threat is less defined and clear, we feel a form of fear called *anxiety*, which is just as uncomfortable but not as helpful. The more complicated the situation, the more are the potential sources for anxiety, and endorphins are not equal to the task of blocking out this kind of pain without help.

The first brief experience of arousal within our brains is pleasurable, and in fact accounts for the intense interest and enjoyment we get from new experiences. If that arousal is prolonged without a break, however, it becomes painful. This is what happens with anxiety. Our attention gets very focused, so focused that we can't break it away to deal with other matters which also deserve attention. Anxious thoughts get in the way of normal activities and remind us of the problems we are still worrying about in the back of our minds. This mental perception of threat sends the signal to the "old brain" to start the fight-or-flight release of hormones again, but with no way to use up the energy they provide. A constant state of arousal is very wearing on our bodies, and can cause any number of physical problems from excessive wear and tear on our stomachs, intestines, heart and other muscles.

As a result, we have developed psychological methods for dealing with psychological pain, in addition to the physical reactions we have been describing. If the body's normal response for dealing with threats is itself causing another threat to our survival in turn, then the prime objective of ensuring our safety and survival must be activated in some other way in order to restore a sense of balance and security. We develop other ways to cope with or ease or avoid or remove the pain, or the threat of pain, so as to defend our health and safety. These defenses have been studied and ranked for how helpful or unhelpful they are in achieving this goal.

But wait a minute—we have many other feelings besides fear and anxiety, don't we? Why is there so much focus on just this emotion and not on happiness, or love, or even anger? Most of us don't spend the bulk of our time quaking in terror, do we? Isn't this view a little lopsided?

We know from experience that we have hundreds of feelings of various kinds and shades and intensities. Anger, for example, can range from mild annoyance through irritation and frustration to rage or even fury. Besides these differences in intensity, there are also differences in overtones of angry feelings. Frustration feels different from the wrath that seeks revenge, which is different from jealousy that combines anger with fear or insecurity, which differs from moral outrage over injustice, and so on. Whole books have been compiled to catalog and describe the various emotions we humans experience.

Besides the many distinct emotions we feel over the course of a single day, never mind a whole lifetime, we also have to consider the fact that we often feel more than one emotion at the same time. We feel disappointment over not getting the raise and the recognition that goes with the promotion at work, for instance, but also feel relief at not having the additional responsibilities and longer hours. The affection and excitement we feel in another's presence may prompt us to say "I love you," but the fear of possible rejection holds us back. We often feel caught in the grip of mixed feelings, or we may be confused as to just what it is that we're feeling about something or someone.

Some mixtures of the basic emotions are so common that they have their own distinct names as feelings: the anger we feel at the inability to complete a planned action which combines with the sadness of not getting to do what we want and maybe a dash of fear that we'll never be able to work the situation out along with disgust with ourselves for failing, goes by the shorthand name of frustration. There are many other "compound" emotions, such as disappointment, jealousy, embarrassment, guilt and love, to name but a few.

So, we have different emotions to wrestle with, sometimes in combination, and at different intensities. Add to this the fact that our feelings are not usually permanent states, but rather are changeable and temporary, depending on the changing information from our surroundings as well as what we do mentally with that information. We change our minds frequently about what we think and what we like and what we want to do; all these changes influence our feelings too, so that we rarely find ourselves experiencing only one pure emotion for any length of time. This is particularly easy to see in children, who can easily be distracted from their distress by changing the subject or directing their attention in a situation elsewhere ("Oh, dear, that's a shame—wow, did you see that?"). Most of the time our feelings are brief and changeable.

Sometimes, however, they blend into a more complex combination that takes into account a number of factors from our environment, and remain more stable over time. These emotional states are called moods, and they last longer than simple emotions, although moods are not etched in stone either and are still subject to change. We tend to name moods either with the name of the strongest or most obvious feeling (a happy mood, a depressed mood), or with a general description of its overall comfort level for us (a good mood or a bad mood). Individual emotions also are often labeled as good and bad, or positive and negative; positive ones being joy, love, satisfaction, and so on, and negative ones being anger, sadness, disgust, and the like.

Calling emotions and moods positive or negative may be actually confusing the issue somewhat, for it implies a judgment that some (positive) are better than others (negative). Strictly speaking, this is not true, for there are some situations in which a "negative" emotion is the most appropriate response. If someone deliberately slaps me, for instance, the natural and normal response is for me to be angry, and there's probably something "wrong" with me—that is, something else that's even stronger than the anger is going on inside of me—if I *don't* feel angry. (What method I use to express that anger is a separate issue.) What the "good" and "bad" labels are really getting at is how comfortable we are when we feel that particular emotion: for most of us, joy feels a lot better than sadness, and anger is physically much harder on our bodies than happiness.

Rating an emotion or a mood on how comfortable it is for us puts us squarely back at the principle of avoiding pain, whether it's physical or psychological pain. So even though our feelings are many and rich and different and intense, they can all contribute to and be influenced by anxiety over the threat of pain, and so are all part of the system of defending ourselves against that pain.

Defending/Coping Methods

A certain amount of pain is inevitable in our lives; nobody can ever have everything they want at the exact moment they want it and in just the right amount to keep from doing any other harm to themselves. Therefore, even babies learn to protect themselves from the pain of wanting something and not getting it, or getting something they don't want, like the babies in the delivery room who can tune out the loud noises. We have lots of ways that we protect ourselves from this kind of pain, all of which can be listed under one of two kinds of options: 1) either we change the circumstance in our environment which is causing the problem, or 2) we change the way we think—or don't think—and feel about it.

If we can change the circumstance, then well and good, and the problem is resolved. I march over to Tommy and take back my toy, and maybe clunk him with it for good measure. I quit my job for one with less pressure or more money. I postpone the picnic for a day with better weather and go to a movie instead. The threat is gone, the pain is avoided, and I didn't need any endorphins to get me through it.

Sometimes the circumstance cannot be resolved, however. I can't choose my parents, or make myself shorter. I may not have the freedom to change jobs because of other factors in my environment. I may be backed into a corner, or at least be convinced that I am, which mentally is almost the same thing. The threat cannot and will not go away. This is the kind of situation which triggers endorphins, but they can't distract us from the pain forever. Sometimes they need a hand in helping us to change our awareness of the threat.

One way we do this is by trying to find other, outside sources for numbing the pain. Chemicals, which have physical as well as psychological effects, are a popular means for achieving this; substances used for deadening pain include not only drugs and alcohol but caffeine and carbohydrates. Physical exercise, which requires a certain amount of focused attention as well as which triggers endorphins of its own, is another common tool.

An alternative method is to find inner resources for numbing the pain, besides endorphins. We direct our attention away from the threat of pain and toward something else. There are a number of ways to do this which have been catalogued by various authors and scientists. Some authors view all of them rather negatively, calling them defenses and implying that any use of them is harmful to our growth and functioning as human beings. Others take the view that these are inborn methods for coping with what would otherwise be unbearable stress, and that their negative impact happens only if they are used improperly, for ignoring problems which could otherwise be eliminated entirely if they got more and better attention. Several of these coping or defending strategies have already come up for discussion in our review of normal human development.

One of the most basic defenses against a painful circumstance which we cannot control or resolve is *denial*. We simply cross the situation out of reality as far as we are concerned; it's not there, it doesn't exist and so we don't have to deal with it. I simply refuse to believe that my cholesterol is dangerously high, and so I don't follow my diet or take my medication. I "know" that my child could not be abusing drugs, so I don't notice the needle marks on his arm. We just blank out those parts of reality which are too painful or threatening for us to face comfortably. This might be a helpful response for the newborns in the nursery who truly are helpless and cannot do anything to shut off at the source the loud noise Dr. Brazelton saw them ignoring. For those of us who are no longer as helpless as newborns, however, using this defense runs the risk of letting a situation that we could have had some positive influence on get worse instead of better, precisely because we are too busy avoiding the pain to see if there is any way to solve the problem itself.

A closely related defense against pain is *repression*. This is more than simple blocking out of some painful event; it's forgetting and then forgetting that we've forgotten it. Whereas denial doesn't let the painful circumstance get in the door in the first place, repression lets it get a toe inside and then kicks it out and slams the door in its face. We prevent ourselves from calling it back into our awareness in order to avoid the pain which comes with it. Sometimes we block out events which were painful themselves: the drunken fights, the sexual abuse, the dark nights when we were left completely alone. Sometimes instead we repress memories of good times which we have lost, because the memories make our current situation seem so much more painful in contrast—we forget the loving intimacy we once shared with our partners and remember only the anger and disgust which give us the extra strength to move out of the house. Repression can be helpful to get us through a circumstance which might otherwise overwhelm us; prisoners of war, for example, have to be able to ignore their suffering and that of their fellow prisoners in order to survive and eventually escape. Even after we have left the overwhelming circumstances behind, however, it is still difficult to surface the repressed memories because repression is a fail-safe system. We not only forget, we forget that we forgot. Repression is among the heavy artillery of our brains' defenses against pain, and we may need some outside help in breaking its grip.

Denial and repression are very early, very basic methods we use to avoid pain or the threat of pain. They try to forbid pain any admittance into our awareness at all. Other defenses focus on sending it right back where we want to think it came from, outside ourselves.

Reversal (some authors call this *reaction formation*) is taking the painful reality and turning it inside out. My baby used to depend on me for everything as her mommy, and her growing curiosity and willingness to leave me to toddle around exploring makes me feel angry and resentful at being abandoned. I certainly don't want to see myself as jealous of a baby, though, so I reverse my anger into overanxious "love" which prevents even normal kinds of exploring—without ever being aware that I was angry in the first place. People who have been kidnapped and are held hostage for a time, especially for political purposes, sometimes find themselves undergoing reversal and beginning to agree with or actively take part in their captor's plans or ideology, at least until after they have been rescued. Changing a painful emotion into its opposite sort of launders it into something that looks acceptable to us and hopefully to those around us. Again, this is not something that we consciously choose to do. We are not setting out to lie or deceive others in order to make ourselves look good. Reversal happens before we are aware that we had the uncomfortable feeling in the first place, as do all of these defending or coping strategies.

Another way to make painful reactions acceptable, especially when it's hard to reverse them into opposites, is to *project* them onto people or circumstances outside ourselves. I'm not angry, I'm merely reacting to your hostility toward me, which don't think for one minute I can't see no matter how much you try to deny it, you're not fooling me one bit! It's as if the others around us are blank screens which receive the image of the feelings we are sending out from inside ourselves, again without ever being aware that we're the light source and movie projector. Seeing a painful emotion or idea as coming at us from the outside, rather than attacking us from inside ourselves, makes it somehow easier to bear because we know we can't reasonably be expected to take responsibility for someone else's feelings or behavior. So we send those feelings out into the environment, and when they ricochet back to us we no longer recognize them as our own.

Blaming others for our own thoughts and feelings in this way is not unlike the blaming that children do to get out of being in trouble with their parents or other authorities. It lets us continue to see ourselves as the good guys who are being unfairly attacked by others. This defense is particularly attractive for some adult children, especially if they were subjected to intense or harsh criticism from an early age and thereby quickly formed the conviction that others are out to trip them up or condemn them anyway. Other people around us tend to resent being set up as scapegoats for our discomfort in this way, however, so the price of using this defense tends to be rather high in terms of loneliness and isolation.

Another common means of coping with things which make us uncomfortable involves letting the painful circumstance inside and showing it to a seat, then shutting the door to that room and not returning. One form of this might be called *selective inattention.* We misplace or forget or lose track of those things that we'd rather not deal with. We oversleep and miss the big final exam; we forget that we promised to weed the garden this afternoon and go play tennis instead. It's not that we deliberately broke a promise or anything, we just forgot! Honest! And that is literally true, since the lack of attention happens without our having consciously decided to do it. Our brains just bypass the information in order to spare us the discomfort of the dread over that overdue bill or that dental appointment. Kids, who have a much less developed memory and sense of time, exhibit this kind of behavior all the time. Adults, who have the physical maturity to remember and to track things over long intervals of time, are much less likely to have a purely innocent basis for constant forgetting of things they don't like. It looks childlike and carefree; it actually is a way of letting ourselves off the hook of dealing with anxiety.

The flip side of selective inattention, as it were, is not noticing what I myself am doing, or *automatism*. I buy cookies and potato chips for the children and don't notice that I store them in the highest cupboard that the kids couldn't possibly reach, while they're not around to see me do it; then eventually I have to eat the goodies all myself before they get stale, since obviously the kids didn't want them. I can pig out with a clear conscience and without the discomfort of guilt, since first of all I bought them for the children and now I'm merely avoiding the waste of perfectly good food. I block out of my awareness the actions I took to set up just this scenario.

A favorite coping mechanism for those who have developed skills in speech and logical thought is *rationalization*. As we have seen in the research on right brain/left brain differences, the left side of our cortex is great at coming up with logical reasons for any circumstance it needs to make sense of. It doesn't guess or express any uncertainty—it just breezes along, making things up in order to fill in any gaps in its knowledge of why something is the way it is. In a normal, uninjured brain, the left half of the cortex has access to the information it needs from the right brain—from sense information, from emotions, from memory and so on—in order to give the true reason for our behavior. If the real reason is too uncomfortable for our self-image, however, and is causing too much anxiety, then the left brain is perfectly equal to the task of making something else up, or leaving out some not-quite-complimentary detail, or otherwise embroidering reality just a little bit in order to spare us the threat of pain. This is not a conscious decision to lie; it takes place out of our awareness, before we realize that we're doing it. It's more like making excuses to ourselves before we had even known that we wanted one.

Most of us can find a way to justify something that we really want to do whenever we need to do so. And since situations are seldom really black-and-white, with only one good or helpful course of action, it may not be entirely bad that we can find solid, logical, rational reasons for more than one alternative for acting in any given circumstance. We need to know when and how to suspend this defense, however, and to deal with alternatives which might be uncomfortable in the short term but improve things in the long run. "Because I wanted to" is a legitimate reason for acting sometimes, provided nobody else is having to pay the price for my decision to act the way I wanted to. We don't always have to dress it up in some higher-toned rationale.

Yet another way we cope with painful reality is by *intellectualizing* about it. We report the facts faithfully, but remove all the feelings which one would normally expect to accompany such facts. The woman who calmly recounts tales of being beaten by her husband, the man who chuckles about his father's drunken rages, the child who never smiles during play—all have split off their feelings from their memories and actions. We take a step back from one half of the reality and turn our backs on it, preferring to deal with just the externals which can be controlled or manipulated like variables in an experiment. The feelings get locked up inside a box, with maybe an occasional nod in their direction but no attempts, ever, to take them out and look at them. At least, we don't look at them as long as we're using this defense, although sometimes in the presence of enough support we can stop walling the feelings off and reintegrate them with the facts again.

One particular form of this mechanism for dealing with anxiety is the use of humor. Comic relief depends on our ability to split normal feelings and reactions from the events which trigger them, to laugh at them instead of crying, and the laughter can provide some relief from the tension and anxiety. It may provide enough relief, in fact, to allow us to refocus our attention on the problem situation and find a way to work it through. Humor can be used purely defensively too, however, as a way to distance oneself from the pain and to keep others a safe arm's-length or more away, without ever going back to the problem itself in order to resolve it.

A last strategy for coping with the threat of pain is *sublimation*, channeling our energy and emotions into socially useful or acceptable directions. Rather than sinking into depression and anger over the injury that cuts short my sports career, I find a less physically demanding sport, or I teach my sport to others, or I lobby for better protective gear, or I work with other injured people to help to rehabilitate them. I use the force and energy of my emotions in a direction which benefits myself and maybe others too, rather than lashing out in fury to merely vent it for the moment. Some authors have gone so far as to attribute all the progress of civilization to the successful sublimation of our instincts to ensure our own individual survival and reproduction at all costs into activities which benefit everyone. At the very least, sublimation allows for more creative solutions to seemingly hopeless situations than the unfocused explosion of emotions and energy would.

We don't have to be codependent in order to be using these defense strategies. They are part of our inborn abilities, built into us as a way of avoiding pain and stress. Adult children may be at a disadvantage for getting past these defenses and getting to the heart of the problem situation or feeling,

Defending or Coping Strategies	
Name	*How It Works*
• compulsive behaviors	numbing the pain by distraction and/or releasing endorphins
• denial	crossing out reality; it doesn't exist
• repression	forgetting to remember what I forgot
• reversal	acting in the opposite way
• projection	seeing my feelings as coming at me from others
• selective inattention	overlooking some important part of the situation
• automatism	not noticing what I'm doing to contribute to the problem
• rationalization	giving a logical excuse for my behavior
• intellectualizing	refusing to feel feelings
• sublimation	finding another way to express the energy of the feeling

however, because they're stuck in a kid's mindset. Kids have not yet developed the mental abilities or accumulated the life experience to be able to tell what is a situation that can be helped and what isn't. The Serenity prayer of Alcoholics Anonymous asks for just this awareness, in fact: "Grant me the serenity to accept the things I cannot change; the courage to change the things I can; and the wisdom to know the difference." The task of becoming fully adult is to learn to tolerate a little more anxiety than we might ordinarily be comfortable with in order to face problems head on and ultimately clear them out of the way for good.

Building Better Skills

Sometimes we are acutely aware of our feelings: at the climax of making love with a cherished partner; as we survey the wreck that is our 10-year-old's bedroom; as we watch the hometown heroes go down in defeat in a close game. We feel waves of strong emotion wash over us at times, and we may fear that they will sweep us away. This feeling of being helplessly overwhelmed is an indication that our limbic system is being activated by memories of past experiences from when we were very young, back before our cortex had developed a sense of time or the ability to reason through how likely it is that an event will actually happen. (Back to that same period in our lives when we were afraid that we might slip through the drain cover and go down the pipes with the bath water.) The "old brain" has no sense of time and so doesn't realize that that was then, this is now; it just knows that this situation feels the same as that one, and makes the match-up. We usually are not aware that this matching of feelings and stored information is taking place, so we don't realize that, say, our present attraction to this person is partly due to his own unique, wonderful qualities and partly due to a number of events and emotions that we experienced long ago and at a time when we were so young in our development that we don't even know that we remember them.

The skills we need to focus on in order to further our emotional development, therefore, have to do with helping ourselves get more aware of what's going on inside us to trigger our feelings, of just what all those feelings are, and of what effect our expression of those feelings will have on everyone who is a part of the situation.

One of the ways in which we develop, which shows up in cognitive development and in moral development, is our ability to take another's role or viewpoint. That is, we learn that others do not necessarily see everything just as we do—in a mental sense as well as in a physical sense. On the emotional level, we learn that while everyone has feelings, not everybody feels the same way about things as we do, or not at the same time or at the same intensity. This happens as we learn that other people are separate from us, not just extensions of ourselves.

Learning that we are separate can set the stage for the development of *empathy*, the ability to understand what someone else is feeling without necessarily feeling that same way myself. I look at the facial expressions and body language of others, watch what they say and how they act, and use this information to get a sense of what they are feeling inside. Research indicates that up to 90% of the meaning of human communication is contained in these nonverbal sources, so this is, in fact, a valid way of getting information.

In order to guess what others are feeling, though, obviously I will have to have some knowledge of what the various feelings are. This means that I also have to be monitoring myself and my reactions to the many situations and relationships in my life, in order to have some foundation for comparing how the other person is reacting with what I do in that and other situations. As a check-up on my guesses as to what others are feeling, finally, I will need to let them know what I'm picking up, just in the off chance that I made a mistake about what I saw, or missed some of the available information. Then they can either confirm my guess as correct, or give me additional information which will let me understand better what's going on with them.

So when I see my friend pound the table, scowl, and raise her tone of voice as she tells me about her supervisor's latest outrageous request, I might say, "You're really ticked off about that, aren't you?" This puts my guess about what emotion she's feeling into a form which makes it easy for her to either confirm or deny it. She might say, "You're darn right, and I've had just about enough of this guy!" or she may say, "Well, actually it's more scary than anything else—I never know what's going to set him off." Either way, I've had a chance to let her know that I'm listening closely enough to get the emotional as well as the literal sense of what she is saying, and she's had a chance to let me know whether or not I understood her correctly. Both of these sides of the exchange help me as I develop empathy.

Note that empathy is not the same as sympathy. Sympathy recognizes the other person's emotional state to some extent, but it focuses on my reaction to it. Empathy seeks only to explore the other person's reaction itself, regardless of how I might feel about it. So, sympathy says, "I'm sorry for your loss" (*I* feel bad); empathy says, "Wow, that must really hurt" (I can see that *you* feel bad). Sympathy, while it is a very fine quality, keeps the spotlight on me and my feelings. Empathy helps me to step outside myself and learn more about feelings in others as well as myself.

When we get bogged down in sad, angry, depressed, or self-defeating emotions, some kind of outside assistance can sometimes be helpful, in order to get enough perspective on what we're feeling to be able to break the mood and get going again. Counselors and therapists, especially those skilled in listening with empathy and trained in uncovering the connections between our self-talk and our feelings, can be of great service in helping us get out of unhelpful habits of reacting to uncomfortable events. Support groups and self-help groups, with or without a therapist as facilitator, can provide much of the same kind of help.

Breaking through the defenses from anxiety is tougher to do, because they do their work outside of our awareness, and it's very hard to work on something you don't even know is there! The classic approach for dealing with defense mechanisms is Freudian psychoanalysis, and it has been effective for thousands of people over the years. Other kinds of therapy and supportive settings can also be highly effective in helping us deal with defense mechanisms, by reducing the overall level of our discomfort. This allows us to take a look at the sources of our anxiety more closely, because we feel safer and less alone. We get helpful feedback from the others in the group or from the therapist, as well as support for our efforts to grow and change what isn't working so well for us.

We are born with a wide range of feelings, but not with the full range of skills for expressing them in constructive ways. As babies, we are helpless at getting what we want, and have no way to alert others to our needs except by raising a fuss. As children, we begin to learn about ourselves and our capabilities so that we can cooperate with others to meet both our needs and theirs. We also learn that feelings are rarely forever, and that we won't die from disappointment or embarrassment. As adults, we must put together all our intellectual learning with our emotional lessons, to put feelings into words in order to take them into proper account as we go through the business of daily life, including its hurts.

We cannot afford to stay locked into howling or throwing tantrums like a little kid as the only way to get across how we feel. We have to transfer all the skills we learn in the various aspects of our human development to those areas where we might be lagging behind ourselves and our capabilities a little bit. Only then can we really be adults emotionally, not adult children. Only then do we really have a choice about when and how and with whom to share all of ourselves, including our deepest feelings. We don't have to settle for the limited options available to infants. When we know where we want to go and ways to get there, even if the journey isn't entirely smooth and without detours, we have a much better chance of actually arriving. And as they say, getting there is half the fun.

The story is told of a sparrow who lived in the Siberian forest in the time of the czars. Usually the sparrow was able to deal with the cruel Siberian winter and find enough food and shelter to make it through to the gentler months of spring. It chanced one year, however, that Mother Nature seemed particularly angry, and the winter winds were unbelievably strong and frigid. The harsh storms snapped at each other's heels, and the sparrow was taxed to its limit to find seeds enough to survive and shelter enough to live through the endless night.

In the depths of January, the coldest month of that dreadful winter, an especially fierce storm blew in. Desperately the sparrow hung in the boughs of a fir tree as the wind relentlessly whipped the branches. The icy needles of snow pelted the bird and it felt itself losing the battle with the elements. Finally it lost its grip and fell to the frozen earth, where it lay still and stiff as the storm howled through the forest.

Hours later a sledge drawn by sturdy horses came through the forest and into a slight clearing. Here the driver paused for a few moments now that the storm had spent its fury, to relieve himself and the horses. As the driver was walking back to the sledge to resume his journey, his foot nudged the sparrow who lay on the ground. The driver was moved to see such a tiny casualty of the storm, and stooped to pick up the bird.

As he lifted the little body, the bird seemed to twitch briefly. The driver felt a stab of hope that the bird could be saved if it could be warmed, but how to do so in the wilderness? The sledge provided no shelter, and the tiny bird would be crushed in the driver's furs as he managed the team of horses. As the driver looked around the clearing, cradling the sparrow in his huge mitts, inspiration came. He gently set the bird up to its neck into a steaming pile of the fresh horse droppings, then took the sledge on its way, whistling with the pleasant feeling of having done what he could.

The warmth of the droppings did slowly revive the sparrow, and as it opened its eyes it could scarcely believe it had survived the storm. The sun reappeared and added its warmth to the sparrow, and life and strength began to seep through its tiny body again. As it recovered, the sparrow looked around and realized with horror where it was. How had this indignity happened? Who could have done *this? They'd better come back and undo it quickly! And the sparrow began to squawk and shrill in protest at his situation.*

In a short time the sparrow heard with satisfaction a crashing through the underbrush, coming closer and closer. He increased his cries. At last, help! They'd better do some fast explaining! A figure came into the clearing and approached the bird. It was a large and hungry wolf who had also barely survived the storm. He grasped the sparrow in his jaws, dunked it in an icy stream and promptly devoured it, then padded off back into the shelter of the trees.

There are three lessons to the story:

1. *Those who get you into it are not necessarily your enemies.*

2. *Those who get you out of it are not necessarily your friends.*

3. *When you're in it up to your neck, it's best to use your energy in reviewing your options to help yourself, rather than squandering it in blaming and causing a fuss.*

Related Readings

Curtis, Robert, *Mind and Mood*, New York: Charles Scribner's Sons, 1986.

Goode, Erica, "Where Emotions Come From," *U.S. News and World Report*, Vol. 110, No. 24, June 24, 1991.

Kent, Jack, *There's No Such Thing As A Dragon*, Racine, WI: Western Publishing Company, Inc., 1975.

Miller, S., Nunnally, E., and Wackman, D., *Alive and Aware*, Minneapolis: Interpersonal Communication Programs, Inc., 1975.

— 7 —

Oh Yeah? What Are You Gonna Do About It?

Kerry is a 34 year old adult child, with a father who is an acknowledged alcoholic who also was fond of marijuana, and a mother who liked to "party hearty." With a work history that includes a series of low-paying, unskilled jobs which don't seem to last for very long, Kerry is equally unsuccessful in relationships. Friends, if you can call them that, come and go awfully quickly in Kerry's life, and as for a romantic partner who knows how to show care and affection, well, just forget about that—Kerry has never felt really loved. Nor liked, really, for that matter, and certainly not appreciated. What Kerry does feel is lonely, and unable to communicate, and confused, and hurt and angry—and often tempted to overindulge in food, or drugs, or sex, or shopping, or anything which will numb the pain for a while.

Kerry watches the talk shows (at least it's some kind of contact with people, sort of, and besides, you learn things) and has heard about codependency. The guests all talk about their disease and their efforts at recovery and how to cope, but somehow they still leave Kerry feeling confused and depressed. Of course you can't help being sick, especially if you caught it from your family, but still, who wants to be an invalid? And that's what a lot of these people seem to be describing themselves as, or something close to it. But then, there seem to be tons of treatment programs and self-help groups around, especially "12-step programs" that are based on the Alcoholics Anonymous model, which we all know has been the most successful program for alcoholics ever. In fact, A.A. has been the only thing that has ever helped Kerry's dad to even slow down on the chemical abuse. So why does Kerry still feel so unsatisfied in a vague sort of way? Is it just denial that keeps Kerry from admitting that codependency is a disease and then seeking treatment? And if Kerry never admits to being sick, does that mean that there's never going to be any hope, or help available for improving the quality of life?

Let's say Kerry starts thinking about codependency in developmental terms, as we've outlined them within this book. What practical effect is this going to have on how Kerry approaches life situations? What real difference does it make if we don't think of being an adult child as being sick?

What If Codependency Isn't a Disease?

There are five characteristics of disease which are listed to prove that dependency (including codependency) fits this model:

1) A disease is describable; it has symptoms.

2) Disease is predictable; it progresses along a set path.

3) Disease is primary; it influences other processes and conditions within the person.

4) It is, or can be, chronic; it doesn't stop.

5) It is, or can be, fatal, ending in death.

Certainly one can argue that all forms of dependency fit this model. An interesting question is, does anything else besides disease share these same five characteristics? What would happen if we tried replacing the word *disease* with the word *development*?

1) Human development is describable; it has stages.

2) Development is predictable; it progresses along a set path.

3) Development is primary; it influences other processes and conditions within the person.

4) It is, or can be, chronic; it doesn't stop.

5) It is, or can be, fatal, ending in death.

Let's examine each of these statements in turn, to see if they are true.

Human development is describable; it has stages. This is the central idea behind developmental psychology, that the process of human growth and maturation is generally the same for all humans. Research seems to bear this out, as does our own everyday experience. In fact, medical science often depends on this same assumption. The stages within various kinds of development have been described in the previous chapters. More technical explanations and descriptions of these stages can be found in the sources listed in the bibliography at the end of this book.

Development is predictable; it progresses along a set path. This is a second assumption of stage theory in developmental psychology, that the stages are orderly and invariant. In other words, we can't skip any phases of development and go back later to insert them. We develop skills and capabilities in more or less the same order as everybody else because that's what it means to be human, as opposed to being some other form of life.

Development is primary; it influences other processes and conditions within the person. This is what we mean when we say that development is hierarchical. The later stages of development build on what has gone before and is already present. Our skills can't be built on air, so to speak. They have to be founded in the selves we are given at birth and continue to fashion as we grow. As we have seen, stages in development in different areas of our personalities (moral and emotional development, for example, or intimacy and autonomy) can interact with each other in order to foster growth in more than one aspect of ourselves at the same time. Some kinds of development, such as in thinking logically, also seem to depend in part on our physical growth and readiness for them. We develop at different rates in different areas because of a number of factors both within and outside ourselves, but we are unified wholes as persons, and all of our development influences our entire selves.

Development is, or can be, chronic; it doesn't stop. While we would be more likely to say "continuous" rather than chronic, the idea is the same: we can grow in knowledge and maturity throughout our lifetimes. This is an idea which has wide acceptance, and the literature on adult development (development which takes place during normal adulthood, coming after the stages of normal childhood development which we have been describing as being unfinished business for adult children) is growing. Most of us see ourselves as open to new ideas and skills no matter how old we may be, and value this as important to a happy life. Although the later stages of human development are not automatic processes which happen whether we want them to or not—we have to choose to continue to grow and change after a certain point—the possibilities for development are always there if we are open to them. Nobody has yet been documented as being perfectly developed to the limit of human capability in all areas of personal and physical growth.

Development is, or can be, fatal, ending in death. Oops, sorry, this one doesn't fit, unless you count life itself as fatal since it too always seems to end in death for us, at least on the physical level. Death can seem to come early for us, however, if we refuse to continue growing to our full potential.

So far, then, the main result from dropping the disease model in favor of the developmental one is that we don't have to see Kerry as terminally ill. But there are other differences in outlook which result from this switch in models too.

For one thing, Kerry no longer seems helpless. If being codependent means being sick, then by the time we find out we have the disease, it's too late already. All we can do is hope to control symptoms, we can never effect a cure. If, however, we are in a process of development—even if we're lagging behind ourselves a bit—we can take steps to catch up to where we want to be. We can be active in our learning and take it as far as we care to go.

Another difference is that Kerry doesn't have to feel guilty or ashamed over past compulsive behaviors. These don't have to be taken as symptoms of a chronic illness; they may be more like the mistakes children make as they grow and develop. Sometimes we screw up as we try to work out a balance between what we want and what we think is right. Guilt comes from the tension between these two alternatives, when we want to do something which we think we shouldn't do. It seems especially intense when the authority to define what should be done is placed in a source outside ourselves.

If Kerry refuses opportunities to grow and to learn how to make better choices, that's regrettable. But that refusal will have consequences of its own, probably in more failed relationships, unsatisfying jobs and uncomfortable feelings. These consequences flow from Kerry's own actions, not from someone else's standards or behavior. Kerry is free to choose when and how to respond to others and to other life circumstances. There is no need to feel guilty when one is making a free choice to act according to one's highest standards.

Kerry does have to be responsible, therefore, but not guilty. Being an adult brings with it the duty to take ownership of one's life and one's choices. Kerry has to make conscious choices about how to live in order to maximize growth and health and happiness, and to minimize pain and sickness and suffering. It is not possible to live a life in which nobody ever gets hurt in some way. Hopefully, Kerry will focus on learning the knowledge and skills needed to reduce the pain inflicted on self and others to the smallest amount. Kerry may feel the need for outside help at some point in order to be able to do this.

Can I Still Use 12-Step Programs?

Nobody grows up in a trouble-free family, not even on television comedies. Some families have had enough trouble handling stress from jobs, health, finances or relationships to be called dysfunctional, and the members of these families are at a particular disadvantage for being able to handle stress and difficulties in their adult lives. In the past ten years or so, a number of self-help groups have been formed to help these people deal with their problems, no matter what form their specific difficulty might be taking.

Many of these self-help groups have been modeled on one of the most successful programs of this type in this century: Alcoholics Anonymous. Its "Twelve Steps" to sobriety and an alcohol-free life have helped millions of people stop abusing alcohol and regain control of their lives and choices. It was this movement which popularized the idea that alcoholism is a disease, not a moral failure or evidence of insanity. It was the first program to offer hope to those who had been unsuccessful in ending their drinking either by medical intervention or by force of will alone.

It was not long after A.A. had gained momentum as a popular movement that the same format of support meetings centered on 12 steps was used to help the spouses of alcoholics cope with the stresses and frustrations of their lives. This, of course, is Al-Anon, and it was followed in due course by Ala-teen for the adolescent children of alcoholics. As the concept of codependency has gained wider acceptance beyond just the field of chemical dependency, those who recognize themselves as adult children have looked for a similar source of support for themselves in battling their "addictions." As a result, there are now dozens of support groups, based on similar principles drawn from A.A.'s Twelve Steps: Codependents Anonymous, Gamblers Anonymous, Overeaters Anonymous, Families Anon-ymous, Sex Addicts Anonymous, Emotions Anonymous, to name only a few. Collectively, these are known as 12-step pro-grams, since all adapt the Twelve Steps of Alcoholics Anony-mous to speak to the concerns of their members.

These groups meet in cities and towns all over the country and in many countries around the world, allowing their mem-bers to examine their actions and to gain insight and support in order to make whatever changes they choose in their lives, so that they regain their freedom to make their own decisions. A fundamental belief which has been heartily endorsed by these 12-step groups is one that they also borrowed from A.A.: that they are victims of a disease process. If we challenge that as-sumption, will we still have the possibility of help from this important source? Can Kerry join a 12-step program without feeling "sick?"

The short answer is, "Sure!" Nowhere in the Twelve Steps of Alcoholics Anonymous, the model for all the other 12-step programs, is the word or idea of disease mentioned. Not even once. The Twelve Steps focus on becoming aware of our pres-ent state, admitting it, getting help from outside resources, making changes in our own lives, and trying to help others who are looking for outside sources. That's a pretty good de-scription of responsible adult behavior in any situation. It's also a fair statement of the goals of human development, since we have to develop our knowledge and skills to at least age-ap-propriate levels in order to be able to do this.

Steps 1, 4, 5, 8, and 10—nearly half of the Twelve—call for the development of self-awareness on our part, warts and all. Insight into ourselves is crucial to the later stages of human development as well. We need to know where we are and

The Twelve Steps of Alcoholics Anonymous

1. We admitted we were powerless over the effects of alcohol—that our lives had become unmanageable.

2. Came to believe that a Power greater than ourselves could restore us to sanity.

3. Made a decision to turn our will and our lives over to the care of God *as we understood God.*

4. Made a searching and fearless moral inventory of ourselves.

5. Admitted to God, to ourselves and to another human being the exact nature of our wrongs.

6. Were entirely ready to have God remove all these defects of character.

7. Humbly asked God to remove our shortcomings.

8. Made a list of all persons we had harmed, and became willing to make amends to them all.

9. Made direct amends to such people wherever possible, except when to do so would injure them or others.

10. Continued to take personal inventory and when we were wrong, promptly admitted it.

11. Sought through prayer and meditation to improve our conscious contact with God, *as we understood God,* praying only for knowledge of God's will for us and the power to carry that out.

12. Having had a spiritual awakening as a result of these steps, we tried to carry this message to alcoholics, and to practice these principles in all our affairs.

where we are coming from in order to set the direction for where we're going. If we combine an awareness of our individual patterns of thinking, acting and relating with a knowledge of the general patterns of human development, we can get a road map for our journey which not only lets us know where we are currently, but points the way ahead. It can alert us to the possibility of pitfalls, and it can point out some opportunities for pit stops. The first skill adults need in order to build better skills is self-awareness.

Steps 3, 9, 11 and 12 talk about taking action in a responsible way to change what we come to see as wrong in our lives. Insight alone is not enough; we have to make changes (that's the literal meaning of *amends*) in order for our lives to really become better. A.A. and its offspring organizations encourage us to make self-directed changes instead of remaining content to react off the cuff, on the spot, at the last second to everything that happens in our daily lives. We are urged and supported to become active instead of reactive. We recover the power to choose, and we own the responsibility to choose wisely and well. This is not just a matter of health or sickness; it has everything to do with growing up.

12-step programs are noted for their openness to the truth wherever their members find it. They adopted the disease model because it has been the most helpful model for understanding dependency to date. The disease model is not built into the Twelve Steps, however, and a developmental approach is entirely consistent with the philosophy of 12-step programs. There is nothing to keep Kerry away from using a 12-step support group, then, if that's what will add the extra boost needed to make changes—even if Kerry doesn't feel sick.

What If I Don't Like 12-Step Programs?

On the other hand, 12-step programs are not necessarily for everyone. Some people are uncomfortable with what they call the "God-talk" of Alcoholics Anonymous and similar groups. Others are too shy to face a whole bunch of people, and prefer to talk one-to-one with others, or to work on their problems in privacy. Some people want a more intensive approach to working on themselves; others don't want to be tied down to anything structured. What kinds of options are available if I can't or won't get to a 12-step program to deal with codependency issues?

Those who like the strategy of working within a support group but want an alternative to a 12-step format have a few other choices. Rational Recovery is a movement which was started in the mid-1980's to provide a different approach to dependency concerns. The meetings and the group's philosophy are based on principles of rational-emotive therapy, the therapy which explores the connection between our destructive self-putdowns, uncomfortable feelings, and our self-injuring behaviors. It is a self-help group, which means that there are no professional therapists or facilitators needed for leading the groups, and members can remain anonymous. Meetings are open, and some members are also members of A.A. Most Rational Recovery meetings focus on chemical dependency, but other meetings centered on other kinds of compulsive behaviors are possible.

Rational Recovery emphasizes the power which resides within each of us to decide how to act and to carry out our decisions. Members expect to belong to the group for about a year as they rework their choices based on the insights they get during the process of membership. They work at recognizing the irrational ideas in the back of their minds which are directing their destructive behavior, and finding more helpful choices for thinking and acting. This process often helps them feel happier and more satisfied as a result. Meetings focus on sharing feelings and ideas. Members are free to exchange names and phone numbers as they wish; there's no formal sponsor system.

The movement started in California but has spread to many states throughout the country, and is beginning to appear overseas as well. Some groups have professionals in counseling or psychology who act as advisors. Members are free to attend as long and as often as they wish; most attend one or two meetings a week, and "graduate" from the program after about a year.

Another self-help group that may be of interest to adult children was founded in 1937, just two years after A.A. This group, Recovery, Inc., focuses on fears and nervous symptoms. Their international headquarters is in Chicago and is managed by members.

Recovery, Inc. teaches its members to change their attitudes, calm their anxieties and control their compulsive behaviors. Meetings are structured: members read a chapter or listen to a tape of the Will-Training method and then share examples of how the skills are helping members improve their lives. There is time for questions and answers, as well as more informal personal sharing between members or in small groups. Meetings are led by members. As with any self-help group, some members may be working with outside professional resources; they are expected to cooperate fully with that treatment as well.

Local chapters of either of these nonprofit organizations are listed in the telephone book, usually in the white pages. Another way to get information on local meetings might be through contacting the community mental health center or community hospital in your area, local information and referral phone lines, or the local headquarters for community fund drives such as United Way.

Some of us are intimidated by the thought of walking into a group of people we don't know to discuss personal problems. We may feel shy, or embarrassed, or ashamed. We may be uncomfortable with more than one or two other persons at a time. Does help for codependency have to take place in a group setting?

While groups are the most common setting for help with adult children's concerns, there are other options as well. Some adult children decide to seek professional help from a counselor, social worker, therapist, psychologist or psychiatrist. Each of these professionals may take a slightly different tack in dealing with the problems. Not only will each individual have his or her own particular favorite theory or treatment approach, there are some basic differences within the various professions.

A *counselor* works to help us achieve more effective personal, social, educational or career adjustment and development. A *social worker* applies knowledge of human development and behavior in the context of social, economic and cultural systems in order to improve or restore our social functioning. A *therapist* may have specialized training in a particular discipline (a psychotherapist in psychology, a hypnotherapist in hypnosis, and so on) and use this knowledge to help us improve our abilities to function. A *psychologist* has advanced training and knowledge in psychology and can offer assessment of our abilities by means of "tests" which may show themes, abilities, or interests which we are not aware of beforehand. A *psychiatrist* is a medical doctor with specialized knowledge about the workings of the mind and the brain, and who can prescribe medication if that is called for during the process of treatment.

Among the schools of mental health which may be particularly helpful for adult children, we have already discussed rational-emotive (sometimes called cognitive) therapy. This approach focuses on the interplay between our thoughts and our emotions, and works to make our moods and feelings more comfortable by rooting out irrational ideas we may be harboring without being aware of them. Another helpful approach which has been explored by adult children is Transactional Analysis, a theory which examines three sources of the messages that we give ourselves about ourselves and our environment (including our relationships); these sources within us are called the Parent, the Adult, and the Child. Transactional Analysis, or TA, tries to figure out what the internal messages are and which source they're coming from, and to keep all three sources in balance for our most effective functioning.

Some adult children find behavioral approaches helpful in changing their previous, unhelpful patterns of acting and relating. These therapies focus on changing our past behaviors in desired directions without necessarily having to first understand where the reasons for those behaviors are coming from. Sometimes insight into the causes and sources of self-defeating behavior comes after having broken the old pattern and trying another kind of action instead. In other words, insight can *follow* changes in lifestyle or behavior as well as *cause* these changes. In addition, adult children find that when they change their own behavior, the hurtful or unhelpful patterns of those around them must change too, because the old ways of relating don't have the same effect on them anymore. Behavioral approaches can be effective in quickly breaking apart self-destructive patterns of acting or relating to others and rapidly improving a bad situation, allowing more time and energy for later insight and understanding on which to base long-lasting and broad-based life changes.

Some kinds of therapies with particular goals in specific areas may be helpful to adult children who want to concentrate on just one area for a short time. Some of us find benefit from focusing on communication skills in order to improve our relationships, or on stress management and relaxation techniques to help reduce anxiety and free up our energy for other concerns. The yellow pages of the phone directory will often list professionals by their area of expertise or specialization to help with locating someone who can address a particular concern we may have. Community mental health agencies can also be helpful in working on specific areas in a short-term format.

Of course, working with a professional costs money, sometimes a lot of money, and maybe Kerry doesn't have insurance to help with the cost of it. Most self-help groups are free or very inexpensive, but let's say Kerry doesn't feel comfortable in a group. With these two strikes already called, as it were, is Kerry headed for an automatic out in terms of getting out of codependency?

Another source of help for Kerry can be found at the library or bookstore. There are many clear, well-written self-help books which lay out strategies for ending old patterns of self-defeating behavior and substituting better plans. There are books which explain human development for kids and adults. There are books on feelings, and thinking styles, and each of the various kinds of therapies which we talked about earlier, as well as many others. You don't have to be a rocket scientist or have a college education to be able to get something out of them. Many libraries also have audio or videotapes on these subjects available to their members. A librarian will be glad to show you where to find what you're looking for, or possibly to get the materials from another branch of the system in some larger areas. The customer service desk at a bookstore will also help you find good books on the subject you're interested in, and can order a special book for you or even tell you whether a particular book is still being printed or not. Bookstores can also be a good source for magazines and journals on these subjects, as are libraries.

Kerry should also be watching the newspaper, radio and television for announcements of public lectures and presentations on these topics. Sometimes an organization will bring a nationally-known speaker to town for their members and make a lecture available to the public at the same time. These are usually low-cost or even free. Kerry may be able to pick up good ideas at the lecture, as well as leads on other books, articles, or tapes which will help with gaining understanding or making life changes. There may be TV programs on local-access cable, besides the talk shows and other programs on national cable and networks. These shows can also be sources for finding out about other kinds of resources which Kerry may want to look up.

So What's the Problem?

With all this help for adult children out there, it may seem strange that we aren't all living happy, productive, worry-free lives already. The final piece of the puzzle is putting things all together and actually doing something about our life choices.

If Kerry wants to take a trip, there are lots of steps to take in order to get ready. Kerry has to decide on a destination and plan the route, get the car checked over and fueled up, pack money, clothing, and recreational equipment maybe, contact friends or family who live along the way or at the other end, arrange for a place to stay, etc., etc. But even if Kerry does a thorough job of looking after all these details and has everything figured out just so, still nothing is going to happen on this trip unless and until Kerry gets behind the wheel and starts the car, or buys the ticket and boards the bus. Kerry has to take charge; Kerry has to act. Understanding how to take a trip is not enough; wanting to take a trip is not enough; planning to take a trip is not enough.

"A journey of a thousand miles begins with a single step." We have to take the steps to move ourselves along the stages of development. We can choose to remain where we are in our lives and our relationships, or we can educate ourselves as to other, better options and go for them. We're grown-ups, we get to pick. We are not, and will never be, guaranteed a stress-free life with no problems, but we will be equipped with better tools for dealing with the stuff that happens, and we will know how to use those tools if we make the effort to learn. Codependency is not forever. We've got a choice.

Once there was a little girl who was very unhappy. She had gobs of homework to do, which she hated because it wasn't any fun. She had chores which were assigned by her parents, which she also hated to do because they weren't any fun either. And she hated the way she looked, because her clothes were all wrinkled and soiled because her room was a mess because that wasn't any more fun to take care of than the other jobs were. "All in all," she thought, "life stinks."

To console herself, she went for a walk by a little brook which flowed near her home. A short way down the bank was a small pile of stones which had tumbled into the water, causing it to burble merrily as it rushed over them on its way downstream. The little girl flopped down next to the stones and began to complain aloud at her hard life and all her many unfair duties.

Suddenly, to her amazement, a tiny figure dressed in mossy green appeared. "It's very tiresome to listen to you whine and complain, little girl," he said.

"Oh yeah?" she retorted. "Then why don't you grant me three wishes so that I could have a better life?"

"I'll do better than that," answered the little gnome. "I'll give you an elf of your very own to get all your duties taken care of. But of course, first you have to prove yourself worthy of this kind of gift. In three days, by the light of the moon, come back to this spot and spin around on your left heel three times. Close your eyes and chant,

'Twist me, turn me, show me the elf!
I looked into the water and saw—'

Well, you'll be able to complete the chant when you look into the stream, for your elf will appear. Meanwhile, go home and complete your homework, so that the elf can have a fresh start when he comes." With that, the tiny figure vanished.

"You might know it," thought the little girl, "getting my wish has some strings attached. Still, I guess it's better than nothing." So she got up, and went home, and started on her arithmetic homework first because she hated that kind the most, and to her surprise she was able to remember most of what the teacher had said and could figure out the rest. Her parents were proud and amazed at how neatly and completely her homework was done that day, and they told her so. The next day her teacher did too.

"Well," thought the little girl to herself, "I've already done what the little gnome told me to do to get ready for the elf. Why should I have to wait three whole days if I'm prepared already? I'll just go back down to the stream and say that chant." She made her way back to the brook and began to spin around on her left foot. She lost her balance and fell into the grass with a plop, and when she caught her breath, there was the tiny green figure glaring at her.

"Didn't I tell you to come in three days?" he demanded. "Can't count too well, can you?"

"That only shows how much you know," replied the little girl. "It just so happens that I got all my homework problems right last night when I tried them, so there!"

"My, my," marveled the gnome. "Who would have imagined such a thing? That doesn't change my instructions to you, however. Go back home until it's time for the elf to appear—and do your chores so that the elf can have a fresh start when he comes." With that, the gnome vanished again.

"Oh, rats!" grumbled the little girl. "I was hoping I'd have help by now for those stupid chores. Still, I guess it will help pass the time." So she got up, and went home, and swept the kitchen first because she hated that chore the most, and she found that if she hummed while she worked it was almost like dancing with the broom. She discovered that she could make a game out of dusting too, pretending she was gliding along in a sleigh over smooth snow, and then polishing the pots became rubbing a magic lamp for a genie to appear. Her parents were amazed and proud at how soon and how well her chores were done, and they told her so.

The next day the little girl grew impatient again for her elf, and decided to go back down to the brook. After all, she had already done everything that was asked of her, and it was only one day early. She went to the pile of stones and whirled around on her heel three times. She began to chant, "Twist me, turn me—"

"What's going on here?" demanded a gruff little voice. "Are you back again already?"

"Oh, come on," wheedled the little girl in her nicest, only slightly whiny voice. "I did everything you told me to. My homework is done, and my chores have never looked this good. And you know, it was easier than I thought, after I got started. Can't I please have my elf now?"

"No," said the gnome. "Rules are rules, and if I let you have your elf early then I have to do it for everybody. Now go home and *wait until tomorrow like I told you in the first place—and clean up your room so that the elf can have a fresh start when he comes." And the gnome vanished as before.*

The little girl was disappointed, but she knew it wouldn't do any good to sulk if nobody cared if she did, so she went home and entered her room, and picked up all her things and put them away, and the room began to look so much better that she dusted and swept it too. And then things really began to look better until she saw her reflection in a mirror as she passed, and realized how dirty and messy she herself looked. So she took a bath, and combed out her hair, and put on fresh clothing and even tied a ribbon around her head. She was amazed and proud at how well she looked and felt when she was finished, and when her parents commented on it, she answered, "I know."

The next day the little girl could hardly wait for the night to come and the moon to rise. She rushed to the side of the brook, spun around on her heel three times, closed her eyes and chanted:

> *"Twist me, turn me, show me the elf!*
> *I looked into the water and saw—"*

and she leaned over and peered into the brook eagerly and saw her own reflection staring back expectantly at her.

"Wait! NO! That doesn't make any sense! It doesn't even rhyme—wait a minute.

> *'Twist me, turn me, show me the elf!*
> *I looked into the water and saw myself!'*

I guess it does rhyme. But it still doesn't make any sense!"
"Oh no?" said a familiar voice. "Think about it."

Related Readings

Berne, Eric, *Games People Play*, New York: Grove Press, 1964.

Hall, Trish, "New Way to Treat Alcoholism Discards Spiritualism of A.A.," *New York Times*, December 24, 1990, page 1.

Schlesinger, Stephen, and Horberg, Lawrence, *Taking Charge*, New York: Simon & Schuster, 1988.

Seixas, Judith and Youcha, Geraldine, *Children of Alcoholism*, New York: Crown Publishers, Inc., 1985.

Suggested Further Resources

Chapter 1: Rethinking the Disease Concept

Dollard, John, and Miller, Neal, *Personality and Psychotherapy*, New York: McGraw-Hill, Inc., 1950.

Kokin, Morris, *Women Married to Alcoholics*, New York: William Morrow and Company, Inc., 1989.

Peele, Stanton, *Diseasing of America*, Lexington, MA: D.C. Heath and Company, 1989.

Szasz, Thomas, "The Myth of Mental Illness," *American Psychologist*, vol. 15, pp. 113-118, American Psychological Association, 1960.

Chapter 2: Intimacy

Ackerman, Robert, *Children of Alcoholics*, Holmes Beach, FL: Learning Publications, Inc., 1983.

Kohut, Heinz, *The Analysis of the Self*, New York: International Universities Press, 1971.

Sullivan, Harry Stack, *The Interpersonal Theory of Psychiatry*, New York: W. W. Norton, 1963.

Chapter 3: Cognitive Development

Ivey, Allen, *Developmental Counseling and Therapy*, Pacific Grove, CA: Brooks/Cole, 1990.

Piaget, Jean, *The Construction of Reality in the Child*, New York: Basic Books, 1971.

Watzlawick, Paul, Weakland, John, and Fisch, Richard, *Change: Principles of Problem Formation and Problem Resolution*, New York: W. W. Norton and Company, 1974.

Chapter 4: Autonomy

Bandura, Albert, *Social Foundations of Thought and Action,* Englewood Cliffs, N.J.: Prentice-Hall, 1986.

Coopersmith, S., *The Antecedents of Self-esteem,* San Francisco: Freeman, 1967.

Erikson, Erik H., *Childhood and Society* (Second Edition), New York: W. W. Norton & Company, 1963.

Horney, Karen, *Our Inner Conflicts,* New York: W. W. Norton and Company, 1945.

Miller, Jean Baker, *Toward a New Psychology of Women,* Boston: Beacon Press, 1976.

Chapter 5: Moral Development

Bandura, Albert, *Social Learning Theory,* Englewood Cliffs, N.J.: Prentice-Hall, 1977.

Fowler, James, *Stages of Faith: The Psychology of Human Development and the Quest for Meaning,* New York: Harper and Row, 1981.

Gilligan, Carol, *In a Different Voice,* Cambridge, MA: Harvard University Press, 1982.

Jung, Carl, *Aion,* in Collected Works, Bollinger Series, vol. 9, no. 2, Princeton, NJ: Princeton University Press, 1959.

Kohlberg, Lawrence, *The Philosophy of Moral Development,* San Francisco: Harper & Row, 1981.

Maslow, Abraham, *Motivation and Personality,* New York: Harper & Row, 1954.

Chapter 6: Emotional Development

Darwin, Charles, *The Expression of Emotions in Man and Animals,* (reprint) New York: Philosophical Library, 1955.

Freud, Sigmund, *The Interpretation of Dreams,* New York: Basic Books, 1900 (first publication date).

Goleman, Daniel, *Vital Lies, Simple Truths,* New York: Simon and Schuster, Inc., 1985.

Chapter 7: Skills Development

_____, *Al-Anon Family Groups*, 1989, Al-Anon Family Group Headquarters, Inc., New York.

_____, *The Dilemna of the Alcoholic Marriage*, 1971, Al-Anon Group Headquarters, Inc., New York.

_____, *Alateen—Hope for Children of Alcoholics*, 1973, Al-Anon Group Headquarters, Inc., New York.

Ackerman, Robert, *Let Go and Grow*, Pompano Beach, FL: Health communications, Inc., 1987.

Berne, Eric, *Transactional Analysis in Psychotherapy*, New York: Ballantine Books, 1961.

Rational Recovery, Jack Trimpey, Director, Box 800, Lotus, CA 95651.

Recovery, Inc., 802 N. Dearborn Street, Chicago, IL 60610.